A sparkling survey of ...

Super Me...
Super Women

Here in a single volume are two of Jilly Cooper's best-selling books: the complete texts of *Men and Super Men* and *Women and Super Women*.

'My only qualification for writing this book is a lifelong interest in the subject. The male – I have found – is a domestic animal, which, if treated with firmness and kindness, can be trained to do most things. It is important to have one in your life to turn on your bath water, do up your zips, carry your suitcases, work out tips, tell silly jokes to, use as a threat when you are having trouble with tradesmen or unwelcome suitors and ultimately to arrange your funeral.

'Men according to legend, want only one thing, are deceivers ever, and are not interested in gossip. They come in all shapes and sizes except for their organs, which according to all the sex books, are exactly the same size when erect and similarly capable of giving pleasure.'

From the Introduction

'Jilly Cooper's is a rare talent that can be achingly funny in very few words'

Birmingham Post

Also by Jilly Cooper

The British in Love
Riders
Animals in War
Class
Violets & Vinegar
Intelligent & Loyal
Super Men & Super Women
Women & Super Women
Jolly Marsupial
Super Jilly
Super Cooper
Jolly Super Too
Jolly Superlative
Jolly Super
Little Mabel Saves the Day
Little Mabel
Little Mabel Wins
Little Mabel's Great Escape
Octavia
Emily
Harriet
Bella
Prudence
Imogen
Lisa & Co.
Hotfoot to Zabriskie Point
How to Survive Christmas
Leo & Jilly Cooper on Rugby
Leo & Jilly Cooper on Cricket
Leo & Jilly Cooper on Horse Mania
Turn Right at the Spotted Dog
Rivals
How to Stay Married
How to Survive from Nine to Five

Jilly Cooper

SUPER MEN AND SUPER WOMEN

(Combining in one volume the complete texts of *Men and Super Men* and *Women and Super Women*)

With illustrations by
TIMOTHY JAQUES

Methuen

A Methuen Paperback

SUPER MEN AND SUPER WOMEN
(This first combined paperback edition of
Men and Super Men and *Women and Super Women*)
first published 1976 by Eyre Methuen Ltd
Second printing 1976
Third printing 1977 (Magnum Books)

ISBN 0 417 05370 3

Men and Super Men first published 1972
Women and Super Women first published 1974
by Eyre Methuen Ltd

This edition published 1982
Reprinted 1989 (twice)
by Methuen London Ltd,
Michelin House, 81 Fulham Road, London SW3 6RB

Printed in Great Britain
by Cox & Wyman Ltd, Reading

Contents

Men and Super Men

TO GODFREY SMITH
In every way a Superman

Introduction

My only qualification for writing this book is a lifelong interest in the subject. The male—I have found—is a domestic animal which, if treated with firmness and kindness, can be trained to do most things. It is important to have one in your life to turn on your bath water, do up your zips, carry your suitcases, work out tips, tell silly jokes to, use as a threat when you are having trouble with tradesmen or unwelcome suitors and ultimately to arrange your funeral.

Men, according to legend, want only one thing, are deceivers ever, are not interested in gossip, like a cosy armful, need two eggs, and seldom wash behind their ears.

They come in all shapes and sizes except for their organs, which according to all the sex books, are exactly the same size when erect and similarly capable of giving pleasure.

At present men are under fire from the Women's Lib movement, which has been described as a storm in a B-Cup, and the biggest bore of the century, only rivalled by the Common Market. One cannot dismiss something, however, because it is boring. Every day through my letter box thunders Women's Lib propaganda: *The Feminine Mystique*, *Women on Women*, *Women under Women*, and so on.

Men in fact have come in for such a pasting that when

I started to write this book, I intended it to be in their defence—my charger and my white plume at the ready. But I found as I progressed how fundamental the antagonism between the sexes really is—how although I love a few individual supermen very deeply, as a sex men drive me up the wall. In fact if there was a third sex, I doubt if they would get a look in from me.

I find I resent the fact that I can't live without them, that they hurt me emotionally, that I hate yet secretly enjoy being bullied by them, that they can do tasks domestic far better than I can, that they enjoy the company of other men so much, and on the whole prefer a bat to a bit on the side.

My husband once went to a cricket week at his old school. I joined him for the weekend, and felt *de trop* from start to finish. I wasn't allowed to have meals with him, or even sleep in the same bed. He was in the dormitory with the rest of the team, while I was allotted one of the boys' studies (alas it was after the end of term) and had to hang my clothes on a row of male chauvinist pegs.

The second evening, bored with my own company and seething with resentment, I walked round the grounds. The air was heavy with the scent of lime trees, the black night blazed with stars. By the pavilion the two teams were having after dinner drinks. Unobserved I sat down and watched them wandering around a little unsteadily, swapping anecdotes, laughing immoderately, rolling up and down a grassy bank, scampering around in a doggy way sniffing out the most entertaining group, forming and re-forming. Away from the tension of the male-female encounter, they looked so young, handsome, carefree, and unguarded as they would never have done if there had been a woman present.

And like the Ancient Mariner, a spirit of pure love gushed from my heart, and I blessed them unaware. The self-same moment, the albatross of my resentment fell from my neck. But it was back with a vengeance as soon as I returned to my lonely truckle bed, and saw all those male chauvinist pegs again.

I have enjoyed writing this book because it enabled Tim Jaques, who did the marvellous drawings, and me to yap about sex every day on the telephone for six weeks. But when we reached the end we decided neither of us ever wanted to look at another man again.

Part 1

This is a book about men—at work and play, in bed and out of bed, in sickness and in stealth. It is also about Superman. Superman is a cross between Charles Atlas and Einstein. He keeps his figure by lifting dumb-blondes above his head before breakfast, and is sent to stud like Nijinsky at the age of twenty-one. The real hero of the book, however, is an individual called Sexual Norm.

Sexual Norm lives in the suburbs. He is married to a wife called Honor whom he has 2·8 times a week. Honor is sometimes satisfied. Norm thinks continually about other girls, but never does anything about them unless it is handed to him on a plate. He is riddled with guilt afterwards. He is doggy, pink faced, with sticking-out ears, nudging eyes, a road-up neck and a fixed avid grin. He blushes easily, laughs loudly, sweats profusely at the back of his neck, and wears dandruffy blazers.

He always has a bath in the morning—just in case—and although he has never dared enter a strip club, if a girl makes him promise not to look he usually does. He is inclined to get out of hand at office parties. His lifelong ambition is to meet a nymphomaniac.

Apart from Sexual Norm and Superman, any man a girl meets will probably fit into one or several of the following categories.

Male Types

THE SERVICES

"I'm bi-sexual—I like Sailors and Soldiers."

Soldiers have yelping laughs and very short hair, tend to have very shiny buttons on their blazers, and never talk about women in the mess. They have broad shoulders and narrow outlooks. They are straightforward and uncomplicated. Occasionally they pounce on the wives of junior officers, but the passes they are most interested in are forty-eight-hour ones. They wear mental battle dress in bed, and fatigues afterwards.

Soldiers tend to be overridden by their wives. Behind most famous soldiers you will find a very powerful dragon who has rammed her husband up the army list as a gunner might force the charge into the breech.

Sailors are always away or having it away. They have far-seeing blue eyes, and there are very few of them left now. Although they have a wife in every port, and two in Cape Town because they stop there twice, nice girls are supposed to love them. Twenty years ago they were considered very glamorous, now they are all trying to get out of the Service and failing to make it in Industry.

Sailors are always rabbiting on about their fine tradition, which as Churchill claimed consisted of nothing but Rum, Sodomy and the Lash.

There is absolutely nothing I can think of to say about Airmen at all.

SCIENTISTS

Scientists have the shortest hair and the thickest spectacles. They wear white coats, talk in whispers, and have never read a book. When they meet a pretty girl they turn pink like litmus paper and have difficulty raising a retort stand. They are all described as brilliant to compensate for being on the non-smart side of the two cultures, and tend to be left wing.

They have a curiously cold analytical approach to women, and are too busy making explosions to have much fire in their bellies.

They are the first target for Rats' Lib.

THE CLERGY

"For what we are about to receive . . ."

In theory the clergy don't—except with their wives or the bishop if he asks them. In fact it is difficult for them to get off with anyone, as unlike catholic priests they don't have the intimacy of the confessional. It must also be a bit turning off to have a whole pewful of parish hats gazing at you with adoration every Sunday.

Perhaps they say: "For who we are about to receive may the Lord make us truly thankful," before they pounce on you, and then send you to the jumble sale afterwards. They are all tone deaf.

DOCTORS

Very easy to get at. Anyone can pretend to have a migraine or pains in the chest. But the Hippocratic oath stops doctors doing anything about it, unless you meet them at a cocktail party or down in the shopping centre. I think most women imagine that because doctors know so much about the female body, they'll be better at making love to it. I should hate to have it off with a doctor in case he found some bump or cavity he shouldn't.

LORRY DRIVERS

Available to hitch-hikers. They make love at 20 miles an hour and have red lights on their rears. They spend a lot of time in lay-bys. A girl friend of mine had a fantasy about lorry drivers in which she passed them a note saying: "You can come home with me as long as you don't speak."

STOCKBROKERS

Stockbrokers play squash all the time—they squash

themselves against women all the way to the City on the Tube, then play squash in the evening to keep their weight down. Later in the evening they play bridge, or go to cocktail parties and shout at girls with flicked up hair and bare foreheads. During the day they make up filthy stories and think about Bulls and Bears.

At weekends they make desperate attempts to be trendy, tripping off to the launderette in sweaters, paisley scarves flowing through a brass ring, their trousers held up under a spreading stomach by a stockbroker belt.

There are very few pretty girls working in the City, which is one of the places to go to if you want to hook a man.

THE LEGAL PROFESSION

Most women, being irrational, will be driven up the wall by the pedantic exactitude of the legal mind. Occasionally a lawyer sends you a legal document covered in kisses, and you really think you're getting somewhere until he tells you he only wants you to sign your name, in three places. And his indecent proposal will be couched in such convoluted jargon, you won't have a hope of defending your honour against him. He will overrule all your objections.

On the whole, barristers are more interested in their briefs than yours. They tend to be pompous and divide you mentally into twelve good men and true when they talk to you. They also put their upper lips in rollers every night, so they can sneer better at their opponents.

TELEVISION (See Fairies)

Men in television brush their hair forwards, and wear white polo-necked sweaters, suede jackets, name-tag bracelets, and deaf aids. They spend their time gossiping—the television centre in Wood Lane is built in a circle to enable the gossip to travel more quickly—and in back-biting—you can recognise a television man once he takes his clothes off because his shoulders are covered in stab marks.

POLITICIANS

Vote Libertine.

Politicians have ringing voices, graciously waving hands, and an all-embracing smile that passes over you like a lighthouse beam. They also make love on all three channels.

Like most men in power they have a hayride sexually—all women wanting to go to bed with a 20,000 majority.

Because on the whole they work so hard, politicians become tremendously randy on the rare times they are off-duty, and because the newspapers are always saying nasty things about them and thwacking them on their marginal seats, they need the reassurance of sexual conquest to soothe their bruised egos. It is very easy for them to be unfaithful because once they're in the House they become completely ungetatable, and their wives never know if they're snoozing on a back bench, chairing a committee meeting or carrying on an affaire of state.

Women, being naturally subservient, are generally

attracted to a man in a position of authority—whether he's a doctor, a psychiatrist, a solicitor who advises them when they're in trouble, a general in time of war, a teacher at night school, a ski instructor, or most often their boss.

SCHOOLMASTERS

Going for a Thong

Schoolmasters however are a very different cup of tea—'children among men, men among children', as Dr Johnson called them. They have chalk in their hair, are dry as dust, hearty, antiseptic, and almost invariably undersexed. They adore the sound of their own voices, and often develop tics and private jokes. Ill at ease in the company of women, they prefer the adulation of a captive audience, their pupils, or the fusty misogyny of their colleagues.

Being accustomed to school dinners, they invariably take girls to awful restaurants. Naturally bossy, they treat their wives like little boys of eleven.

Recommended for masochistic ladies—they are very good at knocking the stuffing out of those smaller than themselves.

FARMERS

Farmers have red faces, purple raw hands and straw in their turnups. They wear long jackets, frequently suffer from calf love, and wear gumboots to keep the sheep steady. They get up very early in the morning and assist in the sexual couplings of animals. In summer they get bitten by insects, and summon milkmaids and landgirls to

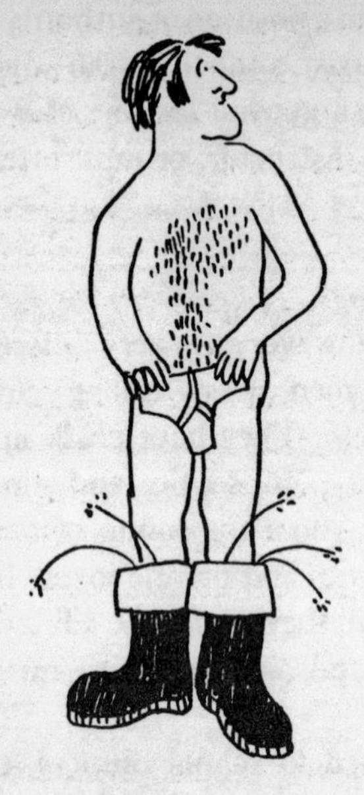

"But I have *taken them off, darling."*

come and see their itchings. Their houses smell of pigs.

Gentlemen farmers spend their time drinking at lunchtime, butchering wildlife, riding in point-to-points and swapping wives. At hunt balls, one glass of bubbly turns them as scarlet as their coats, and soon every cordoned off fourposter is heaving with occupants.

ACTORS

Actors, unlike farmers, get up very late, and go to bed after midnight, unless they are getting up at the crack of dawn to play in some film. As a race, they're inclined to be surprisingly insecure, self-obsessed, only interested in talking shop, and finding out whether Quentin was perfectly frightful at Bristol.

Actors like to make love in front of a looking glass so they can admire their own performance, or with the television on, so they can see how 'perfectly frightfully' all their friends are acting. If they keep their socks on, they're either a blue movie star or terrified of getting foot rot.

On the credit side, they are marvellous at playing out one's fantasies, whether you want them to dress up as a sadistic schoolmaster, a vicar, or a gentleman farmer.

MUSICIANS

Musicians dress very badly, sometimes suffer from Hallé Orchestra and enjoy playing the eternal triangle. Singers however have the most marvellous breath control and can kiss for at least ten minutes without stopping. Trumpeters and any player of woodwind instruments are also very good at kissing, having such mobile lips. Violinists have very versatile left hands—I really dig that double stopping.

Conductors have superb timing: anyone who conducts a whole orchestra shouldn't have much trouble conducting an affaire.

If a man keeps boasting: "Look no hands," while making love to you, he's probably a concert pianist or a brain surgeon and frightened of losing his no-claim bonus.

WRITERS

Writers are alleged to write about it better than do it. Certainly they always regard you as copy, and if you make a *bon mot* while they're making love to you, they'll leap off you and rush away to find a pen and write it down.

However, it is nice to get sonnets from time to time. They also write wonderful letters, which are absolute hell to answer, not much about oneself and full of all those fragments from Donne and Marvell.

One writer I know has an unnerving habit of taking two extra copies of all his love letters, one for himself, the other for the British Museum.

PAINTERS

Painters dress well, and have very nice handwriting. But don't be fooled by that line about only seeing you as a beautiful form not as a sexual object. It's the easiest way I know to get a woman to remove her clothes.

I think on the whole those involved in the arts make the best lovers, for they have more imagination, more ability to cater for your fantasies, and a bigger repertoire. Most of them have a kind of feline, slightly feminine mind—pure heaven from start to fetish. But don't expect fidelity. Art has very little to do with morals.

ADVERTISING MEN

Most of their time is spent making presentations or discussing whether they should insert their eight-inch single column more than three times a week. They dress very well, if somewhat uniformly—navy blue suit, pink shirt—and are generally doused in free sample scent. When you meet them at parties, they say: "Actually I'm in advertising," in a very apologetic way, because *au fond* they feel they ought to get out and do something worthwhile like writing unprofitably, or painting unsellably. Nearly all of them have unsold novels in their bottom drawers and most of them live in Fulham. They have hearts with natural breaks in them.

Stages of Man

Now leaving the professions we move on to some of the stages of man.

YOUTHS (See Schoolboys or Students)

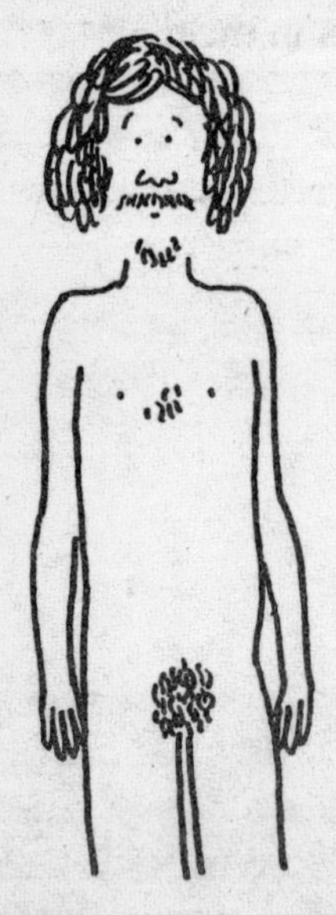

"But of course there's nothing wrong with you, Adrian darling—I just can't stand red hair . . ."

In my youth, youths used to breathe heavily, say thank you three times if you gave them a cigarette, open the matchbox upside down so that the matches cascaded onto the floor, and finally knock over the ashtray.

Today youths are extremely cool, have lean and hungry pelvises and hip measurements in single figures. They often marry at seventeen and refer to their father-in-law as 'baby'. They don't talk if they don't feel like it, but this is probably because in the places they frequent, the music is so loud as to make conversation impossible. They wear clothes which disconcert their elders, including tight jeans to emphasise a bulging crotch. They spend most of their time strumming on guitars or trendy-looking girls who look as though they've just crawled out from underneath a rolling stone. Secretly these girls will worry about tight jeans making a man impotent.

STUDENTS (See Airmen)

OLDER MEN

Peter Pan and Trendy.

It has always seemed unfair to me that no one bats an eyelid if a man goes out with a girl thirty years younger than he is, but everyone starts prophesying doom and desertion if a woman shacks up with a man even three years younger than herself. A woman left by her husband when she is forty either faces living alone or has to break up someone else's marriage if she's going to get married again, whereas a forty-year-old divorced man can have a ball with any dolly he chooses.

As a result the world is now full of seventy-year-old ravers, locks clustering over the collars of their shirts, sideboards laddering their artificially tanned cheeks, and fifty-year-old ton-up boys, forcing themselves into tight jeans, brushing their thinning hair forward, and touching up the grey roots of their jet-black Viva Zapata moustaches. In the evening they wear sawn-off kaftans to hide their pot bellies.

In an attempt to keep up, they exhaust themselves going on vegetarian diets, giving up drink, and dancing all night in discothèques, then going round with grey faces saying they feel twenty years younger. In trying to be Peter Pan, they look more like petered-out pansies.

They also embrace all the phoney mysticism that surrounds smoking pot, and at parties they can be seen going furtively into back rooms and tearing cigarettes apart. Later they gaze into young girls' eyes and say: "My dear, you've made an old man very hippy."

Dolly birds like them—because it gives them kudos in the typing pool to be going out with an older man. Older men can also take them to trendy restaurants younger men can't afford, and are said to be 'experienced' sexually. (I shudder to think what rubbish is dished up in the name of experience.) They also take them occasionally for dirty weekends at a Truss House in Hernia Bay.

FIANCÉS

Fiancés are out of date and not getting it. If pressed they will say: "My fiancée and I have slept together all night in

"Oh for heaven's sake, Harriet . . ."

the same bed, but we haven't actually slept together." Fiancées never give their fiancés their all—only about seven-eighths.

Fiancés have soft curly hair, pink faces from permanently blushing at their predicament, starry eyes, and a mosaic of scarlet lipstick on their downy cheeks from having been embraced by so many new aunts-in-law.

They also manage to appear vacant and engaged at the same time by having a far away abstracted expression on their faces. People naturally assume they are dreaming of the moment when they and their betrothed will be one flesh; actually they are completely shell-shocked by all the talk about soft furnishing and wedding-present lists.

Caught off guard, they have a trapped expression.

As one fiancé said, just before his wedding: "I feel as though I'm going into hospital for a major operation and all the anaesthetists are on strike."

On their desks they have photographs of their fiancées given them by their fiancées, looking mistily soppy in pearls.

BACHELORS

Bachelors begin at thirty-six. Up till this age they are regarded as single men. Most of them are very tidy, smell of mothballs, and have an obsessional old maid's fix about one of their ashtrays being moved an inch to the right. Because they are not married, or living with a woman, they don't feel the need to bath very often. Occasionally they have a shower after cricket and pinch their married friends' towels. They can be recognised by their white underpants. (Married men have pale blue or pink-streaked underpants, because one of their wife's scarves has run in the washing machine.)

Bachelors dread Christmas because they've got so many god-children to remember, and have a very high threshold of boredom through enduring so many grisly evenings with awful girls thrust on them by their married friends.

By way of revenge, they spend a great deal of time sponging off their married friends, turning up for lunch on Sunday and not leaving until the Epilogue, and knocking their disgusting pipes out on the carpet so that they get a chance to look up the wife's skirt when she bends over to sweep up the mess.

They also get wildly irritated by their friends' children, cast venomous glances at a two-year-old, and say: "Isn't it time he went to prep school?"

A married man often rings up his bachelor friend and after a lot of humming and hawing asks if he can borrow the flat to 'change in' that afternoon. When the bachelor gets home in the evening, he often finds various bits of female underclothing, and his bed has been far more tidily made than he left it that morning.

Married friends are also inclined to turn up with whisky bottles, having been locked out by their wives, and spend all night berating the matrimonial state.

It is hardly surprising that although a lot of bachelors

"So *pleased to beat you . . .*"

would like to get married, they cannot bring themselves to take the plunge—like bathing on Christmas Day.

Bachelors can mostly be divided into the following categories:

GAY BACHELORS (See Fairies and Airmen)

ELIGIBLE BACHELORS

They have three address books, and an ejector seat for getting girls out of their flats in the morning. They never have any free evenings because they are constantly being asked out to dinner by designing mums or married women for their divorced girl friends.

MOTHER'S BOYS

"Darling, this is Mummy . . ."

They wear scarves, berets, long macintoshes, galoshes and often work for the White Fish Authority. They always wash apples before they eat them and suffer from hypochondria. When they say they have relations all the time, they don't mean sexual ones, only that they live at home with their mother and sisters.

They have hot milk with skin on it before they go to bed, and read the Lesson on Sunday. People often say they need the love of a good woman, but what they need is the love of a really bad woman to get them off the hook.

They wear camel-hair dressing gowns and grey striped pyjamas. Penalty for pulling the cord is disillusionment.

MARRIED MEN

Let's Play Monogamy.

Married men mostly chat up girls to bolster their self-respect and prove they haven't lost their touch. They are more likely to flash photographs of their children at you than anything else. Although they may claim they're unhappily married and carry on something shocking at parties, they seldom leave their wives for other men.

The confirmed adulterer usually operates from a position of strength: "I'm very much in love with Jennifer, you know. I wouldn't do anything to endanger my marriage, and little Gideon and Samantha mean everything to me."

When you ask if his wife ever gets up to tricks, knowing from the gripevine that she does, he shakes his head smugly and says: "Oh no, Jennifer never looks at another man." (Presumably she does it with her eyes shut.)

I think married people should only have affaires with other married people who know the rules (a sort of: "If you don't leave scratch marks on my back, I won't leave scratch marks on yours"), keep the same hours and are batting from the same position of strength and weakness. There is a freemasonry about married people: they seem to feel it doesn't matter how much they hurt the single person they got entangled with, as long as nothing is allowed to endanger the married state.

But as with older men, it gives a girl terrific kudos in the typing pool to say she's having an affaire with a married man—everyone imagines he looks like Mr Rochester. And the hours are good too. She'll have most evenings and all weekends free, including Easter and Christmas, to run another man.

Younger married men often have their trousers done up with a nappy pin, and black rings under their eyes, not from making love all night but from teething babies. Wedding rings are worn by men who marry foreign girls or who think other people might think they were not attractive enough to get anyone.

Married men of course vary enormously. Some are so henpecked they're absolutely covered in beak-marks, and a burglar alarm goes off if another woman so much as shakes hands with them. Others have what are called adultery toleration pacts, which means they can go off and sleep with whom they like, as long as they tell their wives all about it afterwards. It is all a question of wife-styles.

DIVORCED MEN

"I'm not so old and not so plain, and I'm quite prepared to marry again." W. S. GILBERT.

It always amazes me how vitriolic divorced people are to each other. One girl friend of mine came back from work to find her drawing room piled high with dusty books. Her ex-husband had arrived and taken all the bookshelves away because he'd put them up in the first place.

Another wife stripped her house of all its possessions and moved in with her lover. Three days later there was a knock on the door: it was a special delivery of 400 gallons of water.

"But I didn't order any water," she protested.

"This was the address we were given," said the delivery man, handing her a note. It was from her husband, saying: "You forgot to take the water out of the swimming pool."

Divorced men can be divided into two types: those who left their wives, and those that were left by their wives. If you marry the former, you worry that he's going to do the same to you, if you marry the latter, you worry whether he's still crazy about his first wife, and trying to compete with her. First wives always look like Scarlett O'Hara, or are wonderful little homemakers like Katie in the Ads, who spend their time running up thousands of delicious puddings tasting of Oxo. Or they are boots who don't get married again and cost their husbands a fortune in alimony.

Even if a man's first wife doesn't cast a long shadow, there are always his children to amuse on those eternally long weekends. Scenting weakness, they generally play the

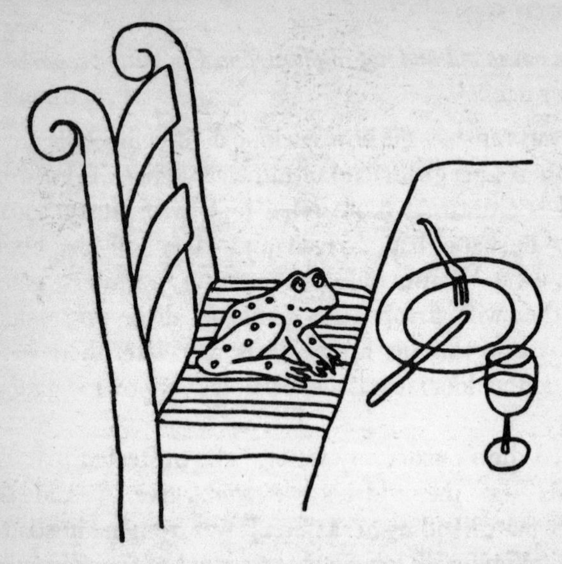

"I got it from a 13th century recipe. Was it all right?"

new wife up shamelessly. If she cooks their favourite food, they say their mother makes it much better. If she plays with them, they get over-excited and won't go to bed. If she tries to suck up to them and buy them expensive presents, they've always got them already.

And then there are those endless dreary afternoons on the Serpentine steering the little mites away from necking couples, or at the Zoo steering them away from copulating animals.

If she's a girl friend rather than a wife, they spend their time telling her how much prettier the girl friend was who came last weekend. Having snapped at them, she remembers they're victims of a broken home and feels guilty.

"Now, come on children, you do *remember Susan . . ."*

Don't catch men on the rebound immediately after they've been left by their wives: they'll sob all over you, and then go off with someone else.

Any girl who is determined to get married should go for a man who's been married six times, and get him into bed. He will then divorce his sixth wife and marry her, being one of those incurable romantics who believes that if he sleeps with a girl he's got to do the decent thing by her.

Divorced men who show no sign of marrying again and appear to be thoroughly enjoying themselves will be a constant source of irritation to their friends, for the men will be jealous and the wives will sense their husbands' jealousy.

Another person who will be disapproved of by society if he appears to be enjoying himself is the lover.

LOVERS

"There always seems something so dirty-sweatered and dirndl-skirted about living with a man you're not married to."

ELAINE DUNDY

Lovers live in unmarried respectability, furnish their love-nests from Co-habitat, and are disapproved of by society, which feels that the man is having his cake and eating it and that both of them shouldn't be avoiding tax. Society is slightly less shocked by men living in sin with girls under twenty-four, because it doesn't feel the man has yet ruined the girl's chances of getting married.

It never enters anyone's head that it might be the girl who is refusing to get married.

Lovers in fact behave far more respectably than married couples. Have you ever heard of a mistress-swapping party? Although they wear their unconventionality in public like a banner, in private they are watching television, washing up and having sex 2·8 times a week like everyone else.

A liaison like this usually begins when a girl is moving flats and wants to leave her luggage somewhere so she dumps it with her boy friend. Before he really knows it, she's moved in, had a key cut, changed the wallpaper in the drawing room, and is adding the usual little feminine touches—bras dripping over the bath, make-up on the carpet. For the first few months they enjoy the thrill of living in sin and playing at being married. The possibility that Daddy might roll up with a horse-whip adds an edge to the situation. Soon other couples are asking them to dinner and they start asking them back, until it becomes a habit.

Men who are living with women are at pains to tell you within five minutes that they are not actually married. On the whole they seem to be more overtly randy than married men just to prove they're not tied down.

SCHOOLBOYS (see Students, Bachelors, Lovers, Married Men, Divorcés)

Class

Class as a subject is as taboo today as sex was during Victorian times. Nevertheless there are still certain differences between the classes.

THE ARISTOCRACY

Sir Galahad everyone in sight

"Open yer legs, dam' yer!"

Aristocrats spend their childhood being beaten by fierce nannies and their later years murdering wildlife, so it's hardly surprising their sex lives are a bit cock-eyed. When they get 'awf' with a girl they automatically expect her to go to bed with them—a hangover, I suppose from the old *droit de seigneur* days. The girl will have to experience a good many *gaucheries de seigneur* first, including a lot of coarse fishing around to find where her bra unclasps. She should be careful if she makes love to him in his own house, or the bedroom door may be suddenly flung open and the general public pour in, having been charged 50p to see over her.

Aristocrats have their mouths permanently open so that the back of their throats is coated with flies like a windscreen after a long journey. They have double-barrelled fowling pieces, wives called Fiona, and never *go* on holiday.

THE MIDDLE CLASSES

The middle class man indulges in wife-swapping parties and swinging—it is all-important for him to keep it up in front of the Joneses. He buys a great many porny books and magazines which he carefully locks away every morning, in case the daily woman finds them. He inconsistently disapproves of what he calls P.D.A.—public displays of affection, or necking in the street. The words 'privacy of one's own home' are often on his lips. He keeps a large box of Kleenex for Men by the bed.

THE LOWER CLASSES

Ever since *Lady Chatterley's Lover*, the lower classes have retained a tremendous reputation for being sensation in the sack—more vigorous and muscular, less fastidious. It's all part of the New Brutality.

Photographers of both the lower and the upper classes are very much in vogue. But the upper class ones have to say 'yer know' every five minutes, and 'ubsolutely funtustic', to show how democratic they are. Photographers have long arms like monkeys from carrying so much equipment about, and usually shack up with models so they can talk shop in bed instead of doing anything else. And they don't have to pay any model fees.

SNOBS

"*I came up the hard way. The lift wasn't working.*"

Snobs or parvenus are very much to be avoided as it's chips on the shoulder with everything. To justify his own insecurity, the snob tries to pull any girl he meets, a case of local boy makes everyone.

His intentions are always honourable: unless you have a title, he will never marry you. What are a few nights of passion to him compared with a lifetime at the wrong end of the table.

I once went out with a Harrovian parvenu. He said: "I fancy you more than any woman I've ever met, but I can't marry you because you're not Upper Class Enough."

I was later irritated to see his smug little face in the Tatler on his wedding day, a horse-faced duchess's daughter on his arm flanked by a battalion of large bridesmaids. Tiara Boom-de-ay. Many parvenus are:

RICH MEN

"*His voice was full of money.*" DOROTHY PARKER.

Rich men are much more attractive than poor men,

beggar men or thieves, but not all that interested in sex. They're too busy training camels to jump through the eye of a needle, and worrying about being down to their last villa in the South of France.

Rich men come complete with all mod cons, saunas, swimming baths, indoor and outdoor barbecues and flagellation rooms. They are marvellous between the balance sheets.

They are funny about money, suspicious of being used, and afraid they are not being loved for themselves alone and all that.

It would be very boring to marry a really rich man, for he'd either be at the office night and day, or else under your feet all the time. You'd spend your life playing tinker tailor with the caviare, and waiting for Jackie Onassis to ask you to coffee parties.

Sexual Types

NARCISSISTS

One of the great misconceptions is that women don't like very good-looking men. They do—the best lovers are either men who cater for and play on your fantasies or who are so beautiful you don't need to fantasise at all. The trouble is that beautiful men aren't usually interested in women.

You also have to spend so much time jostling with them for the mirror, telling them how marvellous they look, and knowing they're only gazing passionately into your eyes to admire their reflection in your dark glasses. And because they feel secure on the basis of their looks, they're inclined to be apathetic in bed.

They are also a bit boring about keeping fit, not eating or drinking much and getting up early to do press-ups. The only press-ups a man ought to do should be on one.

They usually have portraits of themselves in the attic getting older and older, and marry plain women because they don't like competition.

FAIRIES

Every girl should have one at the bottom of her.

One is inundated with so much improperganda these

days that it's easy to think everyone is queer. You can be quite sure, though, if a young man comes floating up to you with flowing locks, gaudy shirt, matching flowered tie, a mass of necklaces, rings on each finger like a knuckle-duster, bells on his toes, clouds of scent, and says "Hullo Baby" in a soft gentle voice, that he's not queer.

Everyone thinks all actors are queer. That's why the straight ones rush round making it with women to prove they're not. I always wonder what the gay ones think when they have to kiss girls on stage: "Shut your eyes, and think of Equity," I suppose.

People automatically assume that hairdressers and antique dealers are queer, but this is no longer so. Since both professions became big business, the butch has moved in.

THE LOUSE BEAUTIFUL

The toast is absent fiends.

Lice Beautiful have accounts at the sex shop, seen-it-all-before eyes, and a million light years of sexual experience under their belts. They also smell of sulphur and brimstone rather than aftershave.

The bounder will love you and leave you, but he'll never put a tongue wrong while he's loving you. If he stuck around you'd find he'd got hidden shallows, that he is the kind of man who has to keep on making love to women because he can't think of anything to say to them in between.

"I'll definitely see you before the weekend, or after the

weekend," he says as he whisks off in his Lotus Elan after a night of passion. Next morning he'll send you two dozen red herrings.

He seldom likes other men, his philosophy being like Byron's, a compound of misanthropy and voluptuousness.

"Hate thy neighbour and love thy neighbour's wife."

TOUCHERS

Excellent well, thou art a fleshmonger.

Touchers cannot keep their hands off you, they must touch flesh and are not safe in taxis. If they're not pinching your bottom, they're propelling you across the road, or putting their hands round your waist six inches too high. If you remonstrate with them they give you a lecture on the importance of grope therapy, and you end up feeling you're both frigid and riddled with inhibitions.

GIGOLOS

Gigolos have the sort of hair styles that make older men snort, pencil in their moustaches every morning and cruise around with For Hire signs on their foreheads. They walk with bent knees because they're so weighed down with presents, gold rings, cufflinks, watches, necklaces, and stoppings.

CASANOVA—the Great Lover.

I've always wondered why Casanova himself was so

"*Harry—for God's sake not* now!"

successful. It must be something to do with stamina: anyone who can keep up a diary let alone anything else for twelve volumes, must have remarkable staying power. Another secret of their success is blanket coverage. They ask every woman they meet to go to bed with them, and though they get their faces slapped fairly often, they also notch up some conspicuous victories. Others concentrate on ugly girls. Nostalgie de la boot, I suppose.

But how many women do you chalk up before you become a Casanova? My husband says 43, which sounds a somewhat arbitrary figure, but he refuses to elucidate. He believes Casanova provides a useful social service, claiming that the best women, like Rolls-Royces, should be delivered to the customer fully run in.

Reputation helps, of course. Once a man has established himself as Mr Rat, women can't wait for him to come along, for they see themselves as the saviour who halts the Rake's Progress. Or as one libertine said of his ex-wife: "She complained I was too well endowed and went on too long, a remark which did me no disservice with her friends."

But what motive drives the compulsive womaniser on to fresher and fresher feels? Like the sportsman who sees a duck flying across the sky and can't resist taking a pot at it, some men have bigger sexual appetites, I suppose, or are frightened of commitment and find safety in little numbers.

The difference between Casanovas and the Louse Beautiful type is that Casanovas like women and enjoy making love to them. "I love the sex," they cry, like Macheath. "Nothing unbends the mind like them."

Whereas Lice Beautiful only take pleasure in conquest. They regard women like Kleenex tissues, to be cast aside once they've been used, or like the pilot who, as the 109th Messerschmitt plunges flaming to the ground, leans calmly out of the cockpit and chalks another swastika on his fuselage.

Some men are promiscuous because they're unhappy, or frightened of growing old and losing their pulling power; others like the brinkmanship of living dangerously.

But promiscuity feeds upon itself. If two women in a man's life are cross with him because he's not giving them enough attention, he invariably moves off in search of approbation and a clean slate, which sets up a chain reaction. Nobody too arouses more disapproval tinged with envy among other men than a Casanova. Empty pots, they mutter darkly, latent homosexual, only doing it because he hates women. No wonder Casanovas get a bit twitchy about their images.

"I'm not promiscuous," said one outraged libertine. "I just like girls."

VOYEURS

Beautiful people looking through beautiful peep-holes.

Part 2

Action

FANCYING

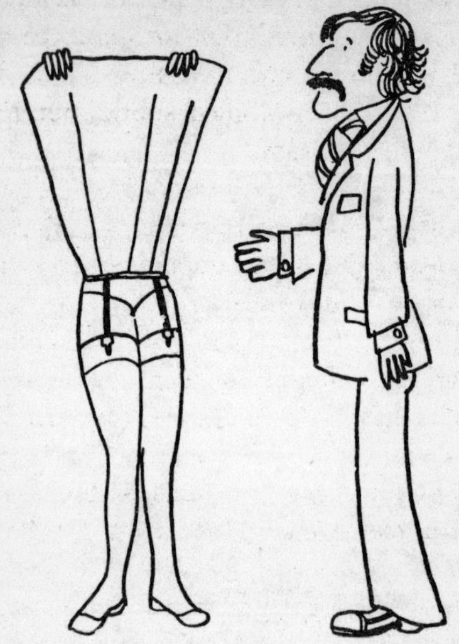

"Tom—do come and meet Cynthia—she's been dying to meet you for ages."

"To think I have wasted years and years of my life, that I have longed for death, that the greatest love I have ever known is for a woman who doesn't please me."

MARCEL PROUST.

I have always contended there are two kinds of fancying. Some men you hardly notice for weeks, and then the whole thing jells like mayonnaise. Others you meet—and it's lust at first sight. But the libido is so irrational. The quality you dote on in one man, you put up with a total lack of in another. Men are just the same.

"I'm a tit man, I'm a leg man, I'm a behinds superman," they cry, and promptly fall for quite the opposite. Ever since I was three, boys have been sidling up to me and saying: "I like my women subtle, but I'm making an exception in your case."

Or:

"My wife likes tailored costumes. I can't really think why I fancy you." Then they quote Herrick's 'Sweet disorder in the dress', and feel better.

And people are always saying: what *does* he see in her? Probably no more initially than a favourable reflection of himself in the girl's eyes. Sexual Norm fancies anyone who shows a glimmer of interest in him. Superman is invariably drawn to some cool ice-maiden, because he wants to ruffle her plumage—it's all part of the untrodden snow syndrome.

I think it's mostly a question of chemistry. People either click sexually or they don't, and if they don't, well, nothing will make a magnet attract a silver churn.

The libido also likes to do its own hunting. That's why blind dates or 'awfully sweet' men people fix you up with seldom work out. I can understand exactly why Chi-Chi and An-An never got off the ground.

Then of course there's the 'Snob'. Proust has a theory that people, particularly women, fall in love in the direction they want to go socially, which is why M.P.s, aristocrats, generals in time of war, and even Prime Ministers and of course dustmen, clean up. The most indolent women have been seen running to catch a boss.

I really fancied an actor I met at a party the other day, but was appalled to find myself rapidly losing interest when someone told me he never got any work. And while we're on the subject of actors, the libido never fails to surprise. Australian women recently voted Peter Wyngarde the man they most wanted to lose their virginity to. Men with big feet are fancied because they are reputed to be well endowed elsewhere.

When a man says a woman isn't his type, it's a polite way of saying he thinks she's totally sexless—but when people say a man has frightful taste in women, it means he's having a ball with girls his friends rigidly disapprove of. Some unfortunate masochists only fancy women who give them a hard time. As Shaw grumbled: "The fickleness of the women I love is only equalled by the infernal constancy of the women who love me."

In fact so much misery is caused by people falling in love with people who don't fall for them, or marrying totally unsuitable people merely because they momentarily fancied them enough to propose, that one cannot help feeling the whole thing is some monstrous legpull, that the Gods are laughing themselves sick up in the skies.

HOW TO MEET MEN

One of the basic dissatisfactions of a girl's life is walking round and round the streets, seeing the most heavenly men wandering about and not being able to get at them. There is not much consolation in the fact that if you met them they might be as boring as hell.

But where do you find men? Oxford and Cambridge

used to provide inexhaustible supplies in the Old Days. One had only to learn to type there, or land a job in one of the colleges, or if you were brainy go to one of the women's colleges, to have a string of men chasing after you. But since National Service was abolished, I am told all the male undergraduates are 'too amazingly young to be any good to anyone'.

There are also more men in the country—because they have to stay where their jobs are—whereas all the girls head straight for London believing this is where the action is. As it is, girls outnumber the men there by about six to one. Most of them end up as secretaries to boring married men, and spend their evenings gazing at the wallpaper in their bedsitters.

You are also supposed to meet men at parties, but how do you get asked to parties if you don't know anyone? Then of course there's evening classes and meaningful glances across the basketwork or the thrown pot—or joining a club, which gives one awful visions of Youth Clubs full of scoutmasters or eager beavers called Stanley with badges on their lapels—or computer dating, which doesn't seem to work much because you can't computerise chemistry and everyone lies like hell. If someone asks you if you consider yourself utterly irresistible, quite irresistible, resistible, or canned nightmare, you are hardly likely to put canned nightmare.

Picking up men in the street or in restaurants is dodgy because you never know if you've landed the Boston Strangler, and there's always the irrational feeling that if he's got time to go round picking up girls he must be desperate, even though you're doing exactly the same thing yourself.

On the other hand it's different picking up men on aeroplanes (on the false assumption that if he can afford a plane ticket he must be rich), on holiday (the same applies) and at art galleries or at concerts (if he loves beauty he can't be all bad). The Tate Gallery incidentally at weekends is one of the best pick-up places in London.

I have also been reading *The Sensuous Man*, which encourages men who want to meet women to hunt them out in the supermarket. Instead of pinching a pretty woman's bottom, a man pinches her trolley 'by mistake' and whisks it down to the check counter. When she rushes shrieking after him, he offers to pay for her groceries, and this way strikes up a friendship. So next time you're in the supermarket, and you see a man lurking, throw a few jars of caviare and peaches in brandy into your wire basket.

Another method the book recommends is for the man to bump into a girl in the High Street and send her parcels flying. He then picks them up, gets into conversation, and offers to buy her a drink to make up for any bruises or breakages he may have inflicted. (This ploy can, presumably, only be used in licensing hours.) It strikes me as being rather extreme—one has visions of the pavements of Oxford Street getting as bad as the M1 in a fog. Perhaps they'll install a Pederasts Crossing for men who don't want to get caught up in the rough and tumble.

THE CHAT UP

"Oh, you say that to all the girls." DICK EMERY SHOW.

Well, he does fancy you and he's decided to do something about it, so he starts chatting you up. You notice the preliminary switching on of casualness, the quick range-estimating glance, the perceptible inner girding of loins, or squaring of shoulders. Sexual Norm straightens his Club tie, smooths his sweater down over his bottom, pulls in his stomach, whips off his spectacles, crinkles his eyes engagingly, and puts on his goat *fatale* face. He then goes upstairs, brushes his hair, and starts all over again.

"Please, Mr Elmhurst, put me down this instant!"

Usually a man indicates his interest in you by shooting you a penetrating glance, which you return and hold just a second longer than is polite, as you say: "Whoops tra la, here we go again." Soon your eyes are meeting so often in penetrating glances it doesn't matter that you've got nothing to say or he's talking about garden sheds.

Superman, when he's chatting you up, never lets his eyes swivel to see if there's something more amusing behind you, he howls with laughter at your weakest joke, and remembers what you've said an hour later.

He only leaves your side, even if he's given every chance of escaping, to go and fetch you another drink, so he can shoot you a long-distance smoulder across a crowded room, then bolt back to your side again. He keeps telling you how pretty you are, which works a treat—all women like a bit of buttering-up with their bed. Occasionally he touches your hand when he lights your cigarette. Sexual Norm, in an attempt at sophistication, puts the cigarette in his own mouth to light it for you, and hands it to you all soggy.

A lot of men chat up girls by being rude to them. But personally I don't fancy the plain blunt type. If a man's likely to put me down, I don't let him pick me up in the first place—I like soft soap, a flannel and a duck for my bath. My idea of an agreeable man is one who agrees with me. Nor do I like a man who boasts of his conquests. If he's keeping open bed for half London, what's in it for me?

As he is leaving, Superman moves into action:

"We must meet again sometime." (Smouldering glance.)

"We must."

"Where can I get hold of you?"

"Wherever you like, darling." (Smouldering glance.)

"No, I meant your telephone number. We must have dinner sometime." (Lunch if either of you is married.)

Superman then memorises the number until he gets

outside the room, when he writes it down. Sexual Norm overhears and jots it down in his diary, alongside the addresses of hundreds of other girls he's never had the courage to telephone. In fact, knowing he's got her number and could ring her up lessens his desire to try.

THE DATE

"And afterwards, Miss Dyson, you might like to come round to my place . . ."

My experience has been that men who are interested ring you up within twenty-four hours, and ask you out.

I get very irritated when they telephone and say: Guess who. I always guess wrong deliberately. Nor do I like men who ring up at twelve o'clock and say how about lunch today, giving you no time to wash your hair or appear faintly unavailable. Or, when you don't want to speak to them, give someone else's name, Omar Shariff or Sean Connery, to get you to the telephone. Even more maddening is when they call you and keep you on slow burn by chatting you up for a quarter of an hour and then don't ask you out.

I don't like it either when men, having got your address, drop in uninvited at all hours of the night expecting an ecstatic welcome just when you've gone to bed covered in cold cream and rollers. This is a fundamental would-be-seducer's error. Nothing makes a woman less sexually receptive than feeling unattractive.

For the first date, any man who's worth his salt will spend a bomb on dinner, the theatre, etc. Equally, the girl who is worth his assault will spend a bomb on a new dress, shoes, make-up, and at the hairdresser's. Sex is expensive.

Most courtships seem to be carried on in restaurants, helped along by soft lights and hard liquor.

Superman never takes a girl on public transport—the lighting's so frightful. It's either cars, taxis, or a short walk (and I mean short), if it's not raining or freezing, under the stars.

ON THE FIRST DATE, MOST MEN TAKE YOU TO A RESTAURANT.

Superman gives you plenty to drink, doesn't translate the menu from French for you, or spend so much time chatting up the *patron* and asking the waiters about their mothers that he's got no time for you.

"Darling, I'm so hungry I could eat you."

He also arranges for you to sit side by side on a bench seat at a decent distance from other people so that he can brush your hand with his occasionally, or even put a hand on your thigh when he's making a telling point.

"I definitely think Arsenal" (playful pummel) "are going to win the cup."

On a bench seat too, it's much easier to make eyes at other people if you get bored.

If you sit at a table opposite a man, you miss half his sweet nothings, you've got nowhere to look if there's a lapse in the conversation, and you're quite likely to waste the whole meal playing footy footy with a table leg.

Another point to remember is that if your dinner-date chooses what he's going to eat with infinite care, then eats all three courses, he's not really keen on you. It's those untouched plates of food that indicate a grand passion.

Meanness of course is a great turn-off. Those men who say: "I thoroughly recommend the grape-fruit, they sugar it awfully well here, and why not have pasta for a main course?" afterwards expect you to pay for your dinner horizontally. The same type always fails to conceal that he's keeping the bill afterwards, and if he takes you to a party first, encourages you to fill up on the canapés so you'll only need a very plain omelette later.

Lunch I have always thought is an even more erotic start to an affaire than dinner. When you have the enforced discipline of getting back to the office or the children, you always come on much stronger than you would normally.

OR YOU CAN TAKE HER TO A PUB.

Sexual Norm usually takes girls to his pub on the first date, because it's cheap, because his friends will be impressed if they see him with a girl, because there's someone else to talk to if he runs out of conversation. And he knows where the Gents is.

I'm not wild about pubs, they're all right in their place but not for courting, with all those bursts of well lubricated laughter, and large men in sports coats wanting to break into song. The bar stools are just the wrong length for my legs, and if you collar a table someone always comes shuffling over clutching a glass of lager and a cheese roll, sits down and inhibits your conversation.

Invariably too your date drinks pints of beer, when you have a gin and tonic, and as you finish long before he does, if you're polite you hide your glass, or if you're like me, you rattle your ice or ostentatiously eat your lemon peel to encourage him to buy you another.

Pubs however are infinitely sexier than Indian restaurants: nothing could be less turning on than flocked wallpaper, bright lights, glasses of warm light ale, a meat vindaloo-flavoured kiss afterwards, and onions, which recur through the night.

Going to the theatre is nice for a first date—as long as you choose something jolly and the man doesn't spend the whole time grumbling that there's nowhere to put his legs. You should also dine afterwards rather than before.

Cinemas are all right too—but here again you should dine afterwards with plenty of alcohol. There's always something faintly depressing about the return to reality: your date doesn't look quite as good as Steve McQueen, and you certainly don't look so good as Jane Fonda. Horror films are excellent because they're good for a giggle, and you've got a marvellous excuse for pretending to be frightened and clutching each other.

THE PASS

Sexual Norm by this time will be treading out the ground for the pass. We all know the tell-tale signs: the slowing down of a car on a lonely road, the hand edging along the back seat, the manoeuvring into an empty office in the lunch hour, the sidling up on the faded rose-patterned sofa accompanied by a murmur of: "Are your flat mates really out?"

The girl if she fancies the man is wondering how much and how soon she can give in without feeling cheap.

Norm has been known to pounce from the arm of a girl's chair, and be rudely deposited on the floor when she leaps to her feet.

A lot of men reluctant to face a rebuff, make verbal passes.

"Can I come up for coffee?"

"Does your husband ever go away?"

"When are you next going up to London?" (This to a country wife.)

"I thought next time we lunched it might be fun if we had a leg of chicken and white wine at my flat."

"The grass really isn't wet, you know."

"Our bodies do talk the same language, don't they?" (This one usually on the dance floor.)

Or the more direct but less subtle approach: "I fantastically want to fuck you."

Sexual Norm, who realises the importance of being a good sexual conversationalist, sometimes says: "Would you mind awfully if I kissed you, Jennifer?" and then lunges even if she says no.

It must be difficult being a man. If you pounce too soon everyone calls you a wolf, if you hold off too long everyone calls you a queer. If you make a pass of Khyber-like proportions at a girl who fancies you, she'll say you're wonderfully passionate, if you do exactly the same to a girl who doesn't, she'll complain you're mauling her.

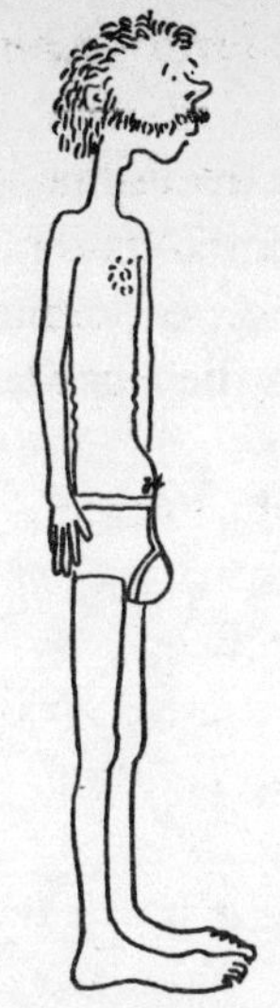

"Big feet, darling . . .?"

In theory, Superman is never in a hurry. His timing is so good that he always waits to make a pass at you at exactly the moment you're worrying he might not—so you plummet like the proverbial ripe plum into his arms.

But the whole pass-making business has become such a game—the man waiting until you're getting worried, you falling over backwards not to appear worried—that it all goes on until you both go off the boil.

Other men are so impervious to the come-on signs that you don't know if they're genuinely shy or just playing hard to get. They're so reserved you wonder if someone else has reserved them already.

The smooth operator of course, who always prefers to

play on home ground, lures you back to his flat. Soon you're lying on his sofa without your shoes. The central heating is up, the lights are dimmed, soft music is spilling into the room, and out of the corner of your eye in the next room you can see the most enormous double bed covered in furs. Within minutes the zips are down.

* * * * *

Bed

"Sex isn't the best thing in the world, or the worst thing in the world, but there's nothing else quite like it."

W. C. FIELDS.

LOCATION

Once a man knows a girl's interested, where does he take her? It's all right if both of them have got a flat—but if they haven't there's all the hassell of packing a suitcase to spend a few hours at a hotel, or borrowing a friend's flat to 'change in', or waiting till nightfall to do it in the back of a car, or for summer to do it in the long grass.

Wives always say they couldn't possibly commit adultery in their own house, but lust is a great leveller.

Superman books a room at the Ritz and launches the girl into a sea of vice with a bottle of champagne, ordering smoked salmon in the interval. He believes in mixing pleasure with pleasure.

I've often wondered why smoked salmon is so erotic. Perhaps because it reminds one of rather warm bare flesh.

Before he was married Sexual Norm used to commit fawnication (sic) on a creaking single bed. The girl invariably bumped into the landlady on her way to the bathroom on the next floor.

Some women with marvellous figures like to be undressed before they leap into bed. And for this reason boys ought to take a course in undoing bras at prep-school. But with most people it's a race to get undressed

"But Angus, I always thought one never *wore anything underneath . . ."*

and into bed before the other person has time to see their stretch marks or spindly calves.

Bachelors sometimes take their clothes off and fold them up in polythene bags. Older hippies get undressed in another room, so they can remove their corsets in private and return with a swish of terry towelling.

Adulterers look in the cupboard or under the bed. Superman takes the telephone off the hook. He also has a fire extinguisher on the wall in case the girl bursts into flames.

Once in bed both parties breathe deeply and say "A-a-a-ah" several times. This is usually construed as ecstasy, but is in reality because of the coldness of the sheets and other people's hands.

People always try harder with new people. Sexual Norm will spend the next ten minutes worrying whether he's giving the girl enough sexual foreplay or fiveplay, and then grimly thinking about cricket or football to keep his mind off sex. He occasionally says '*Howzat*'.

The girl, remembering what the sex books told her about not lying back and being passive, will be frenziedly stroking Norm's neck, tickling his toes, kissing his navel, and putting on such a display of acrobatics that he has to try and think even harder about cricket or football.

Finally with the words 'there are no frigid women, only incompetent men' ringing in his ears, Norm starts threshing away like a sewing machine that's got out of hand.

THE BLAND LEADING THE BLAND

Then come the lies.

The man, crossing his fingers, will say: "I don't do this very often, you know."

The girl, crossing her legs, will say: "Neither do I."

He: "I've only been to bed with, er, five women in my life."

She (uncrossing her legs): "This is the first affaire I've had since I've been married."

He: "I wouldn't dream of going to bed with a girl I didn't feel deeply about." (Feeling deeply under her dress.)

Several asterisks later he will say: "That was wonderful, darling. Was it wonderful for you, darling?"

"Gosh, that was marvellous, darling. Was it wonderful for you, darling?"

I'm sure one of the reasons for the permissive society is because girls wear so few underclothes these days and are more getatable. Whenever I went out with a new man—fifteen years ago—I used to buy a new pantie-girdle to keep my curves at bay, which acted as a complete chastity belt. And, even worse, there were those all-in-one corselettes, which totally denied access.

MULTIPLE BOREGASM

Sex books in fact have made Sex absolutely impossible. Havealot Ellis and the still small voice of Kama Sutra were all right, but recently I was sent a book consisting of 287 pages devoted to Oragenitalism, which needed a degree in engineering to be understood. And you can go crazy trying to memorise all the refinements of *The Sensuous Woman.* "The Velvet Buzz Saw, the Butterfly Flick." Nor can I see that it honestly adds anything to your sex life if you suddenly disappear in the middle of a steaming session to get chocolate ice-cream from the fridge to smear all over each other. And think of the laundry bills.

I'm sure all those ludicrously controlled positions they advocate are responsible for the high incidence of slipped discs these days. I wouldn't be surprised if most sex books were written by osteopaths to encourage business.

"Oh damn, I've lost the place again."

Cosmopolitan magazine the other day was exhorting girls to excite and cajole their lovers with wildly obscene language. Sexual Norm, who's been brought up not to swear in front of a lady, would be absolutely horrified.

In fact after reading a sex book manual, I'm amazed any man dares pounce on a girl at all. He must be so worried about 'ejaculatory incompetence' or being a tower of jelly in a crisis, or not being able to come ten times a night. Then there's always the problem of having wined not wisely but too well. Of the four stages of drunkenness: jocose, bellicose, lachrymose and comatose, it is essential to catch the girl at the post-jocose stage.

And novels are so sexy too these days that even if a couple are having a quiet read before going to bed, the girl is liable to become insanely amorous just after the man's taken his sleeping pills.

LUST IS THE MOTHER OF INVENTION

I'm a believer in lust—if two people fancy each other silly, they usually have a nice time in bed without the aid of chocolate ice-cream or the Velvet Buzz Saw.

Of course there will be men like the Old Man of Thermopylae who never did anyone properly, or lazy men, who believe in labour saving vices, and just lie on their backs and let the girl do all their work.

But on the whole I think the good lover has a way with women as some people do with horses—he makes them relax, he creates the kind of cosy emotional atmosphere in which a woman is not afraid to ask him to do the thing he wants to her. He is also an enthusiast, he cares for making a woman happy rather than making her, he is not frightened of getting his feet or anything else wet—relief would be just a lovely wallow away.

I don't think most women are crazy about sexual athletes. If he can twist you into every position in the Kama Sutra that's gym not sex. Nor are they wild about marathons. The third day he rose from the bed may be all right for some, but it's no good if he doesn't press the right buttons.

Finally the most important thing in a good lover is a sense of humour. He should be someone who can send the whole thing sky high, who wouldn't mind if you were having an off day or didn't feel up to it.

"But sweetest, why in the bedroom?"

BATHS

Afterwards lovers are supposed to have baths together, which I've always thought was an overrated pastime, particularly if you sit at the wrong end and have the taps digging into your back, with one side scalded and the other one frozen. On the other hand if you don't have a bath together, whoever has last bath not only has to make the bed but also clean the bath.

THE VENERABLE BIDET

Then of course there's the bidet—somehow if you go to someone's house and see a bidet in their bathroom you assume they must be sexually switched on, or French.

MEN AND SUPER MEN

Sexual Norm thinks bidets are for bathing the dog. American girl in Paris hotel: "Dig that crazy drinking fountain."

VASECTOMY

According to a recent article this is the most beautiful thing a man can do for a woman; it's also one of the shrewdest. If a man has a vasectomy, he can have an absolute hayride sleeping with anyone he wants to without danger. His wife however is completely stymied if she suddenly gets pregnant.

DIRTY WEEKENDS

"But, darling, when you said a dirty weekend . . ."

Dirty weekends are divided into two kinds, the first when both the man and the woman intend to sleep with each other, the second when the man is intending to sleep with the woman.

As the former usually take place in hotels, the couple's main problem is to appear married, because if the hotel staff rumble the fact that they are not married they may easily try to put one of them in the Annex. A girl friend of mine recently spent a dirty weekend in Scotland, punctuated by dour Highland Ladies banging on the bedroom door and crying: "Come out, come out."

"Oh for goodness sake, Annabel, we've got to leave early in the morning."

The couple should therefore remember not to roll up in separate cars with separate luggage bearing different names. They should also not appear too animated at mealtimes, but gaze gloomily into space like other married couples. The girl should also remember not to ask the man whether he likes sugar in his coffee at breakfast or what name she should put in the register.

One wife I know after her husband had spent a dirty weekend in the Cotswolds with his secretary found the bill in his name. When taxed, the husband told her it was his partner's bill. "The swine always uses my name when he gets up to any of his tricks." The wife believed him, and went round saying what a louse her husband's partner was.

If a girl goes on one of the latter dirty weekends when the man is trying to make her and has promised there are no strings attached, he usually invites her to stay with married friends who immediately steer her into a room with a large double bed, which they claim is their only spare room. Or he will take her on a boat, and not until it's at sea, does she realise it only sleeps one.

Love

LOVE

"*If you believe in me, I'll believe in you*"

ALICE IN WONDERLAND.

"*I am melancholy when thou art absent, look like an ass when thou art present, wake for thee when I should be asleep, and even dream of thee, when I am awake; sigh much, drink little, eat less, court solitude, am grown very entertaining to my self, and (as I am informed) very troublesome to everybody else. If this be not love, it is madness, and then it is pardonable.*" The Old Bachelor.

A great deal of time is spent kidding oneself a man is keen on one when he isn't. Once a man is hooked he will:

find every one of your idiosyncrasies endearing

roar with laughter at your most inane jokes. (People in love sound like hyenas)

write you letters, when he's going to see you the next day, which he tears up

bore all his friends talking about you in the tones of gross hyperbole

lose interest in everyone else

telephone all the time

make heroic efforts to spend every moment he possibly can with you to the extent of driving you 30 miles home after a date, picking you up from the office to take you to the station, or crossing London in the rush hour for the sake of being with you for two minutes.

Men quite often behave like this to a girl before they get her into bed. If they act like this afterwards, she's on to a good thing and should stay on.

NORMAN'S SEXUAL CONQUEST

Being susceptible, Norm falls in love about three times a year. At present he is hooked on a well stacked typist in the office called Dental Floss.

His wife Honor can always detect the signs. She hears Norm yelling for clean underpants in the morning. She then watches him putting deodorant between his toes, cutting himself shaving because his hand is shaking with excitement, shrieking with agony when his new French Aftershave gets into the cuts, leaving a snowfall of talcum powder on the bathroom floor, and cutting his toe nails surreptitiously into the waste-paper basket instead of in bed as usual.

He then polishes his shoes, changes his mind five times about what tie he's going to wear, picks the only rose in the garden for his buttonhole, spends hours combing his hair over his bald patch, and can be seen slipping a toothbrush into his briefcase. Sometimes he cleans his teeth.

Honor notices he has also taken to carrying cigarettes and a lighter although he doesn't smoke, and spending a lot of evenings at regimental dinners or out with the boys and returning completely sober. When she rides in the car she finds her seat belt has been lct out to accommodate a vast bust.

FOR EVER AMBER

Some men are so filled with caution, they can never bring themselves to propose. I've seen so many girls go out for years with a man in the hope that they might hook him in the end. They spend their time looking for signs: "He's talked about our going on holiday together, he's going to get a house when the lease of his flat runs out, he's taken me to meet his mother, he's got my photograph in his wallet, I've looked in his diary and he's got nothing but squash with Geoffrey and cricket fixtures for the next six months." But the man still won't say he loves her or ask her to marry him.

The girl becomes more and more bitchy and resentful, even though she knows she's not furthering her cause. Men like to come home to someone restful and neutral who doesn't make scenes.

Or she resorts to the awful boredom of playing games, flirting with other men to keep her man on his toes, or rather on his elbows.

If only she had the courage to break it off. But it's rather like trying to get out of a tepid bath, the water is getting colder and colder, but it's still warmer than the cold outside.

Some girls try and shove a man Gretna Green-wards by showing him what a grand little home-maker she is, mucking out his flat, washing his shirts and rugger shorts, being fantastically good with all his married friends' children, currying favour and chicken leftovers. But I don't think it works.

"Well, I just thought we could go out after all . . ."

I'm against Women's Lib because I think women come unstuck when they do the chasing. They can't keep the beseeching or the stammer out of their voices when they ring men up. Then there is the expense of giving a whole cocktail party, in order to extend a casual invitation to one man, who probably doesn't come anyway, or asking a man to dinner and filling the place with so many flowers and candles it looks like a funeral parlour.

Now most young men are far more house proud and domesticated than girls. They live in bachelor flats with all mod cons. They shop at the late-night supermarket, and their washing is done for them by the dragon in the launderette who has a soft spot for men. Their shirts drip dry over the bath. They have no difficulty in getting a char.

In the kitchen in the evening they know all about basil and tarragon as they whisk around in their butcher-boy aprons, blinding you with domestic science. They are even marvellous at washing up. Gone are the good old days, when indulgent wives used to say: "Norm's a wonderfully imaginative cook, but it takes me three days to clear up the pots and pans after him."

As they listen to the Women's Lib screeching, men must wonder why they should bother to marry at all, and get terrible complexes about enslaving a suffering female, or turning a graduate into a cabbage. They don't need wives to darn their socks or the holes in their arguments.

THE COOLING-OFF PERIOD

Nothing is sadder than to feel a man going off, it's like trying to hold water in cupped hands.

The coward usually does it with a kiss, and then stops ringing up. If he starts saying things like: "I'm awfully *fond* of you, Jennifer," or "I love you but I'm not *in* love with you," or "We don't have much in common except the obvious thing, do we?" Or if he's married: "I think Honor suspects something, so perhaps we'd better cool it for a month or two"—you know the end is very near.

Personal Habits

HYGIENE—ME AND MY FIVE O'CLOCK SHADOW

"Well, it's quicker than a bath any day."

Television advertising has made us positively paranoiac about hygiene. A man hardly looks at a girl without fretting whether he's forgotten to use his roll-on deodorant, his anti-perspirant, his Lifebuoy Soap, or his

Gold Spot. A lot of his time will be spent shaving twice a day so he can dunk himself in aftershave, cleaning his teeth, worrying about the Y-fronts and Wherefores of Under Stains, and lobbying to have a bidet installed in the office Gents.

The sweet smell of success has been replaced by the success of sweet smell. If a man smells remotely rancid you can assume he hasn't got a television, or only watches B.B.C.

I like men to wear scent. I hate mouths like mossy caverns and I prefer fur coats to furlined nostrils. But it is very turning off if a man stops his car and starts crunching Polos, before he crushes you in his arms and fills your mouth with peppermint-flavoured splinters.

The nicest men taste faintly of garlic—but not of onions.

Sexual Norm, who wants to get his teeth into Dental Floss, is wondering whether he ought to get circumcised because he's heard it's more hygienic.

CLOTHES

Once upon a time there were hard and fast rules about what a gentleman wore. But recently the young have raised two fingers at fashion, and now anything goes as long as you wear it without selfconsciousness, and with style.

One was always being told that no gentleman would wear rings on anything but his little finger, or coats with belts, or suits without a tie or braces—but somehow with shoulder-length hair they all look perfectly all right.

I'm still not wild about jerkins, or knickerbockers, or any kind of hats, baggy flannel trousers, lovat-green cardigans or white polo-necked sweaters on older men trying to look younger ("a touch of white is so flattering near the face when you get beyond a certain age").

I'm also allergic to shorts except on athletes, belted camel-hair coats, vests, and gloves except on ski instructors or gynaecologists. And I can do without the anorak brigade, and old school ties—that awful idea of looking at someone's neck first to see if he's acceptable.

It also amazes me how few men have a sense of colour.

"Your HAT, Charles."

They don't seem to realise that grey looks hell with a sallow skin, and red with an English red-brick complexion.

Or, as a chum of mine said who went to see a friend in prison: "Brown simply isn't Gordon's colour."

Well dressed men always seem to get someone else to wear their suits in for them. Sexual Norm wears a blazer with a Rotary Club badge, a club tie with shields on it, and a battery of fountain pens in his breast pocket which leak onto his white nylon shirt when he presses himself against girls.

HAIR

Very few Englishmen seem to realise the importance of having their hair cut properly.

They also seem to have no control over their barbers.

"But, Celia, I'm working until 3 every morning. How do you expect *me to get it cut?"*

Having just grown their hair to a reasonable length over their collars, they suddenly start muttering about having too many wisps round their ears or the older men in the office looking disapproving, and disappear to their barbers. They emerge with their sideboards shaven, absolutely non-existent back, front and sides, and looking just about as gruesomely sexless as soldiers used to on their first leave from National Service.

It takes at least two months for them to be bearable to look at again.

I can't think why they're so reluctant to grow their hair. Not only is long hair pretty, it also covers a multitude of sins, such as an ugly hair line, a dirty neck, protuberant or dirty ears, and carbuncles.

Dreadfully square men who fancy themselves often have it cut short at the back but slightly longer at the front, so that it curls on their foreheads and makes them look boyish.

BEARDS

I'm not wild about beards on men or women, particularly if the men have very full red lips, or their beards are always getting clogged with soup, cream or melted butter. I suppose if you shut your eyes you can fancy you're being kissed by some furry animal who might be Jupiter in disguise.

The Common Market

THE COMMON MARKET

In the next few years, the country will be flooded with foreigners, Frenchmen who would a-wooing go, Italians who take every remark you make with a pinch of flesh.

Wives will greet their husbands with the question: "Had a good Dago at the office, darling?"

When I was eighteen I spent a fortnight in Majorca with a girl friend. The beauty of the Majorcan men affected us like a fever and they soon returned the compliment. The first day we sat on the beach we suddenly became aware of hundreds of small, dark, handsome men edging inch by inch towards us on their stomachs like an army on manoeuvres, and soon we were surrounded. Every night we seemed to go out with at least six men.

After a few days my friend settled for a flamenco dancer, but I couldn't make up my mind between a taxi driver and a telephone mechanic called Angel, until one evening the taxi driver took me for a long walk along the beach. A huge white moon had turned the sea to gunmetal.

The taxi driver removed his coat and hung it on a breakwater, then took my scarf and spread it out on the sand. How like Sir Walter Raleigh, I thought, very moved, and was preparing to sit on it when I was firmly pushed out of the way and he sat on it himself. He was damned if he was going to have his new suit covered in sand. After that I settled for Angel.

What other single men is a girl likely to get off with on holiday? Sexual athletes from the Gorbals in their prehistoric shorts and their sandals and socks. Pallid Belgians in snorkel masks, airtubes and flippers looking like something out of Doctor Who. Germans who spring 100 yards across a crowded beach to light your cigarette. Danes so impossibly blue-eyed and beautiful that they couldn't be interested in women at all.

Beware too the French gigolo with his curls and flat stomach, his flashy crawl and his superb English. If you spill Ambre Solaire on his shirt, he'll drop his accent in a trice and turn out to be some hairdresser from Palmers Green.

Even the stolid English wolf will find his sheep's clothing too hot on holidays and emerge in his full colours as Playboy of the Western World.

When he gazes deep into your eyes and murmurs: "Let's spend the rest of our lives together like that ah, um, you know, that classical couple who spent their lives together" he doesn't mean it. Holidays produce beautiful ephemeral relationships but rarely husbands.

Angel the telephone mechanic turned up in England that winter. Without his suntan, without a job, but with gold teeth and a shiny suit, and speaking no English, he was a far less attractive proposition.

When Sexual Norman goes on holiday he gets drunk on the B.E.A. flight going out and sings 'Valencia here I come'.

Man and his Recreations

MAN AND HIS RECREATIONS

"I'd rather he had his hobbies than other women."

I think a lot of male-female resentment stems from men spending so much time away from their beloveds—not even earning money, but spending it instead in clubs, pubs, or playing games.

THE CLUB

One of the last bastions of male chauvinism. Not only do they discriminate against women but also against each other. If you are Jewish or foreign and want to get into one of the more august clubs, you have to change your name not once but twice in case they ask you what your name was before you changed it.

If a wife rings up to speak to her husband, the call is taken by the porter or the steward who puts his hand over the receiver and asks: "Are you in, my Lord?"

After lunch at a boys' school, dining in one of the ladies' annexes is about the most unglamorous thing in the world. Awful décor, overhead lighting, cress on everything and musty waitresses called Dolly with indiscreetly dyed hair. The ladies usually consist of a few felt hats, and their pale daughters fingering their pearls and about to go back to school.

HIS FRIENDS

"Darling, you must meet Leo and Roger, my oldest *friends."*

"Some of my best friends are friends."

One of a man's most irritating habits, along with revving up his car when he thinks you ought to be ready, leaving one sock in his trousers and talking about time and motion when he watches you doing housework, is showing off in front of his friends. He only has to be surrounded by a few cronies to start making snide remarks, about you but more likely about your friends. If you take him to task at the time, you will be accused of making a scene. If you bring it up later, he will have forgotten what he said, and accuse you of making a mountain out of a molehill.

One of the silliest things one is ever told as a gel, is to avoid men who haven't got any men friends.

HIS CAR

"Yes, definitely a big end . . ."

Cars are a complete sex substitute. Why else do men refer to the beastly things as 'she'? Let a carman into your life, and you will be woken every morning by the squeak of chamois leather, or be stood up on a date because he's 'moving cars' this weekend. Carmen howl round the shopping centre effing and blinding at every traffic light, wear awful gloves with holes in the back, rush up to anything with a strap round its bonnet and pat it as though it had just won the Grand National, and are so used to lying underneath cars that they always take the underneath position when making love to you, and then complain your big end's gone. Beforehand they wind you up with a starting handle.

On the coldest day in winter, they put woolly hats with pom-poms on, and drive you for hours with the hood down to blow the cobwebs and your wig and everything else away.

In the summer as a treat they'll take you to Silverstone where you will stand pressed against a railing surrounded by men in flat caps talking about gaskets. Occasionally a car flashes by making the sort of noise that unpleasantly resembles a dentist's drill, and a voice says "that was Old Graham", or Jackie. If you say you admire a certain driver, it's always someone who, it turns out, kicked the bucket last week.

A few years ago, sports cars were the thing, but now I'm glad to see they have been replaced by Rolls-Royces with blacked-out windows. Riding in them you always think the weather is much worse than it is, and feel very cheerful when you get out.

BOATS ARE EVEN WORSE

Sailing is absolutely terrifying. You arrive for the weekend all dressed up in brand-new old clothes with your hair just done, and as soon as you set sail a dirty great wave rolls up and absolutely drenches you. Next moment, the sail is lying on the water, and the darling amiable man who asked you on the boat has turned into Captain Bligh and is yelling blue murder at you. Something about going aft. The nicest men become absolute monsters once they get a bit of string between their hands. Most of your weekend will be spent in the hold, cooking meals which everyone throws up.

The amazing thing about sailing is that although by day the men bellow at you and can't tell the girls from the buoys, at night everything changes. The boat is moored, the whisky comes out and they're all ready to seek out your Jolly Erogenous zones and play deck coitus. If there is another couple aboard, you are bound to have changed partners before the weekend is out, for there is something about lack of space, appallingly uncomfortable beds, and seasickness, that makes people incredibly randy.

GOLF

If you go out with a man who plays golf, your biggest problem will be not to laugh the first time you see him in action. Once they get on the course, the most sober, steadfast and demure individuals suddenly blossom out like court jesters, in the most brilliant colours and fashions—lemon-yellow caps, pale-blue anoraks, cherry-pink trousers. And when they wiggle their feet to get their stance right they look exactly like cats preparing to pee.

Their language is even more colourful. My uncle had a house near the fourth tee in Yorkshire, and all his children had to wear ear plugs.

In the club house afterwards they will suddenly start kissing your hand, downing gins and tons, asking you what's your poison and saying haw, haw, haw all the time.

Golfers never have one night stands—they hole in one.

RUGGER MEN

Here comes Thunderthighs.

Rugger can be the most romantic game in the world—

who could resist Gareth Edwards? It can also be the most boring, if you're watching on the touchline in the icy cold and it's Harlequins 42, H.A.C. nil.

After the game, having covered themselves with mud and glory, rugger players spend hours and hours in the bath, and then expect you to talk to other rugger wives while they down pint after pint of beer. Occasionally in the back of a car, they will make a forward pass at you.

If you marry a rugger player, you won't get sex on Friday night in case you put his eye out, all the towels will disappear, and by the end of the season his suitcase of kit no longer needs carrying, it walks by itself.

Rugger players love orgies, because they remind them of the scrum.

"But Gilbert, I played front row last *night . . ."*

ROWING MEN

Row me oh, oh Row me oh.

HORSEY MEN

Goodness, she isn't wearing a bridle.

Horses and sex seem to go together. If you've got something between your legs all day, you want to carry on in the same vein at night.

Horsey men have tough faces, vice-like thigh muscles (although that may be an illusion created by their jodhpurs), and figures of eight engraved on their bottoms from sitting on so many shooting sticks.

They will tighten your girths before they mount you and pin a red rosette on you afterwards. Never make love to them upside down or the luck will run out of them.

SHOOTING

Hearing about shooting is very tedious, with all those Harris Tweedledumbs who roll up at a girl's flat with a bloody grouse in each hand and proceed to twelve-bore everything but the pants off her, telling her about their exploits on the Glorious Twelfth. Going shooting on the other hand is rather fun—like walking under armed escort—as long as you make sure the guns stop for a long boozey lunch in the middle of the day.

Between each drive you will hear rather ambiguous cries:

"Where's Rufus?"

"Picking up birds in the woods."

or

"Hey, that's my cock you've got hold of."

The guns work off so much aggression being beastly to their dogs that they're usually quite nice to women.

BRIDGE

Definitely addictive—people who are short on conversation or old before their time play bridge—and once hooked they would rather play than take a girl out. All bridge players sweat heavily.

FOOTBALL

I've never actually met a football player but 'Match of the Day' is an absolute godsend. It's the only time you will have free to wash your hair, or pluck your eyebrows —your man will be absolutely glued to the box. Watch out for Action Replays, though.

Orgies

ORGIES

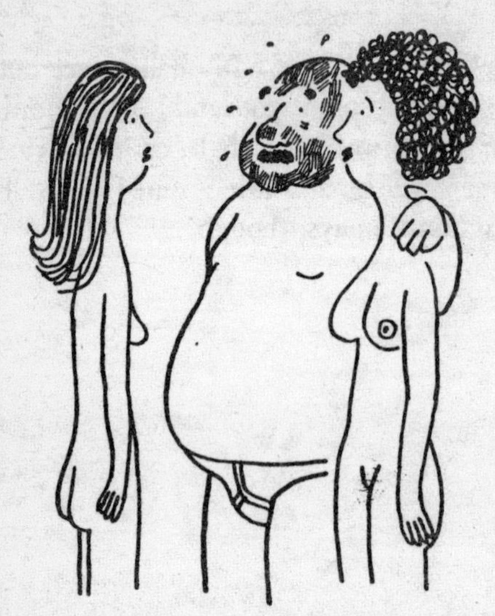

"Er yes, yes, Miss Weldon, the matter of your overdraft will be quite *all right . . ."*

Two way mirror on the wall, who is the barest of us all?

Very few people will admit they've been to an orgy, and those who do say they only watched and it was very boring. "No central heating, and not enough to drink," said a male friend of mine. "And lots of bank managers in their underpants talking about cars. It was rather like having a bath with one's Nanny. Not much fun and nowhere to look."

This is a far cry from one's fantasies of pulsating wall-to-wall couples, people in sheets drinking wine out of goatskins, girls coming out of pies and crushing black grapes with very white teeth, and sophisticates with jaded parrots watching through two-way mirrors.

I'd be a dead loss at an orgy, for I'd be convinced everyone in the room was looking at my awful feet. In order to participate I'd have to drink myself silly, and as soon as I drink myself silly I feel sick and am a write-off sexually.

But I'm fascinated by the ethics of orgies. Do men come up to girls they want to couple with, tap them on the shoulder, and say shall we lie this one out? And to get everyone going, do they say: last man in works the gramophone? And do they have Ladies Excuse Mes? How awful too if no one asked you and you were a floor flower all evening.

If Superman goes to an orgy, of course, it's like the first day of the sales, with all the women trying to get at him. Sexual Norm however, although he is excited about loving dangerously, is worried about his wallet and the size of his member, and is still in his Y-fronts. He tries to look like a film producer, hoping that the starlet in the corner might be the sort who wants to get to the top on her back.

Dental Floss, who is looking skittish in Woolworths pearls, exhorts him to strip.

"You've got nothing to hide," she says.

"That's what I'm afraid of," says Norm. He watches her rush up to a trio of car salesmen.

"You three can have a body like mine," she cries.

Norm looks across at his wife Honor, who is still wearing her roll-on and talking about deepfreezes to another housewife. Norm decides he's really much better doing it with Honor. He wishes he was completely hairy up to his waist like a satyr, then it wouldn't show if he took his underpants off. It must have been easy for satyrs in the old days. He wishes he could go home.

Next day however he will regale his friends in the pub with a torrid account of the mountains of heaving flesh, adding: "I really didn't know where to put myself."

"Come again?"

Women and Super Women

TO ILSA YARDLEY

With love

Introduction

You may ask—not unreasonably—what excuse there can be for adding as much as a jot to the wordy flux that has poured off the presses in the last few years on the subject of the female sex. Can it be that there yet remains a syllable unuttered on the topic of 'unpaid domestic servitude', or some unignited spark of controversy over the locale of the female orgasm?

The Female Ghetto, *The Sensuous Eunuch*, *The Ascent of Women* etc. etc.—the only thing these joyless outpourings have in common is a dreary ability to take themselves too seriously and an infinite capacity for grumbling about the female condition.

Only a couple of decades ago there was a universally hummed popular song called *I enjoy being a girl.* Today, in the mid-seventies, Jan Morris was practically lynched for saying the same thing.

In fact in turning from man into woman, Miss Morris has gone very much against the tide, for the most depressing aspect about women today is that so many of them seek to be becoming more and more like men. One sees them wearing trousers the whole time, cutting their hair short, storming the stock exchange and the civil service, taking over men's top jobs, taking the sexual initiative, refusing to do more than a minimum of housework, paying someone else to look after their children.

The hand that is stretching out to rule the world,

seems no longer to have any desire to rock the cradle. Gone are the days when girls were dear little things exclusively manufactured from sugar and spice.

Women, as we knew them, in fact, are a rapidly vanishing phenomenon in grave danger of extinction. Conservationists fretting over the fate of the rhinoceros or the butterfly should immediately turn their attention to rescuing the female, if only to preserve her in Wild Wife Parks or Bird Sanctuaries before it is too late.

I felt it was essential before the sex became extinct or disappeared in a pouffe of smoke to get down on paper details of the female's behaviour pattern, her hobbies, her breeding and brooding habits, and also to categorise the physical characteristics of the various sub-species: nymphomaniacs, Tory ladies, virgins, debutantes, lady cricketers and many more.

The result was *Women and Super Women*. And Timothy Jaques, who did the drawings, and I sincerely hope that this little monograph may be placed beside the dinosaur skeletons in the Natural History Museum, as a memento for future generations of the days when the female sex still roamed the world.

Woman proud woman clad in little briefs. . . . I shall no doubt be accused of being too harsh on my sex. But I would like to protest like Macheath, if perhaps for different reasons, that I love the sex: "Nothing unbends the mind like them."

I am constantly amazed by their beauty, their vulnerability and above all by their intrinsic sillyness even when they are at their most serious and tub-thumping. All women are good, as the proverb says, for something or nothing.

Women and Super Women was written very appropriately in longhand in the pages of a publisher's dummy (a book with blank pages) for *The Gathering Storm* by Winston Churchill.

As we hurtle towards gynocracy, and the strident howls of the Women's Liberationists become more clamorous, I doubt if the battle of the sexes has ever raged more bitterly. But before they take over altogether I think women should perhaps heed Sir Compton Mackenzie's words:

"Women do not find it difficult nowadays to behave like men; but they often find it extremely difficult to behave like gentlemen."

The Ages of Women

SCHOOLGIRLS

Schoolgirls write endless letters to schoolboys scented with Goya's Great Expectations, which progress from Dear to My, Very Dear to Darling Darling Darling as the term passes. Status is entirely dependent on how many Valentines they get. A lot of wishbones are wasted on Paul Newman.

During the school term schoolgirls smoke like chimneys but don't inhale, smuggle in pornography and spend a good deal of time asking more sexually experienced pupils: "What's it like, what's it really like?"

During the holidays they lie on the floor, play pop music too loudly for their parents' liking, and keep transistors under the bedclothes so they can listen to Capital Radio all night. A lot of time is spent reading beauty advice books about not squeezing blackheads and drinking P.L.J. Occasionally they make out lists of every part of their body, and launch heroic campaigns to make each part more beautiful.

Schoolgirls are supposed to be filled to the brim with girlish glee, but are actually permanently in despair because there is no possibility of Paul Newman or anyone else who looks like him ever loving them back. Meanwhile Paul Newman and thousands of men who look like him are having fantasies about nubile schoolgirls.

TEENAGERS

Teenagers have spots, puppy fat, immortal longings, sleep all day, and worry about kissing properly, whether they're exchanging too much saliva or going on too long, or whether they should be stroking the back of their boyfriend's neck as they do in films. When they first progress to French kissing all they can think of is how disgusting the underneath of men's tongues feels.

All teenagers live in jeans with mottoes embroidered all over them, which are evidently a great icebreaker: you read each other's private parts and suddenly you're friends. To quote from one teenage magazine:

"He had *Beauty is Truth* down one side of his jeans and *Abandon all hope ye* on the crutch and the sort of smile that labelled him a very real person."

Most teenagers are very keen on someone called Mousy Tongue.

They change at least three times a day, and spend three hours on their faces before coming downstairs, in the hope that one of their father's friends will chat them up, or a group of workmen will whistle at them in the street. They also stuff Kleenex into their bras, giggle a lot, spend all their money on *Movie Magazine*, *Jackie* and pop records, and wonder why they can't marry Paul Newman. After all, Juliet was married at fourteen, wasn't she? Permanently Spock-marked, they believe the world owes them a living, and stay in jobs only three weeks.

Other occupations are slamming doors, having wild parties when their parents are away, smashing crockery from pre-menstrual tension and pinching their mothers' clothes.

"She's got a man, and she's past it, what does she need with clothes anyway?"

To get their revenge, mothers often hang around when their daughters have friends in, cramping everyone's style when they want to neck and talk about sex.

Teenagers are also intensely irritated by their parents continually grumbling about money, but still spending fortunes on drink.

VIRGINS

Per Ardor ad Asterisks.

Almost a collector's item these days. Virginity is supposed to be something you give your husband like engraved cuff-links on your wedding day.

When I was a gel girls kept fantastically quiet if they lost their virginity, now they get panicky if they haven't lost it by the time they're twenty-one.

Virgins are permanently under siege from Herrick urging them to gather rosebuds, which is a euphemism for losing it. They worry that once they've lost IT they're going to want IT all the time. They know they're saving IT for something, but are terrified that it's getting too late, and soon, no one's going to want IT. Virgins also worry about the pain on

"What d'you mean—lost it?"

their wedding night, but so much will be going on, rockets exploding, asterisks, the breaking of waves and Ravel's Bolero in the background, that they'll be completely distracted from any pain.

Girls who have lost their virginity often move to other parts of the country so they can pretend to be virgins again.

One's mother and one's daughters are always virgins and have children by internal combustion.

DEBS

Red Eyes at night, Deb's delight.

Debs live in the General Trading Company, are all called Fiona and Georgina, wear headscarves on the chin to keep their mouths from falling open, have high clipped little voices, never dye their hair and fornicate like stoats. They also wear trousers that don't fit, carry Gucci bags with another scarf attached to the handle and wear flat shoes with tongues and chains.

Much of their time is spent grumbling to the newsagent that the latest copy of the *Tatler* hasn't come in, eating their way through five-course charity dinners in aid of the starving, and working as "sekketries" in offices, where they get on surprisingly well because they talk to everyone in an attempt to prove that only the middle classes treat the lower classes badly.

In ten years' time, their hair will be tucked inside a petalled hat, red veins will be springing on their cheeks, and they'll be wearing exactly the same clothes that were fashionable when they were Debs.

FLATSHARERS

You tend to see them most on Fridays, again with suitcases clutched in their hot little hands as they surge towards bus stops in South Kensington and Knightsbridge, on their way to offices where most of them work as rather imperfect typists.

On the bus they will shout across to one another about "Dominic and Gideon and those two perfectly super medical students we met skiing."

Their suitcases, which block the cubby-hole under the stairs, contain a week's dirty washing for Mummy and a smart little dress in case there's a drinks party, or a smart long dress in case there's a hunt ball. Most of the weekend will be spent sleeping off the rigors of the week: a week of jousting for men, gossiping with other girls, rowing because Samantha hasn't cleaned the frying pan, and eating scant suppers off big knees in front of hired television sets.

These are the Guardswomen of S.W.3. London is the battleground and men are the prizes. Here in bathrooms festooned with drying bras and tights that drip like some Chinese torture, they will soothe their battered minds and bodies in tepid water from some rusty boiler that would put Heath Robinson to shame.

Here they will sleep in a bedroom not unlike the dorm at school. They have come to London because they've been told that is where the action is—most of them are a little bewildered to find they aren't having a more madly gay time.

Girls who share flats seldom have much in common except a desire to find a mate. They probably came together in the first place because two of them went to the same school, or their mothers did, and a third or fourth were needed to pay the rent.

Fed on a diet of *Woman's Own* and Barbara Carthorse, much of their time is spent reading their horoscopes or wishing on the New Moon: "Oh find me a husband, a Prince Charming to whisk me away from this Squalor to St James, Spanish Place."

Men visiting the flat are seldom allowed in the bedroom, not out of modesty, but because they would be so appalled by the mess: clothes everywhere, spilt make-up, a week's supply of coffee cups gathering dust under the bed. And yet from this squalor, elegant and beautiful girls will regularly issue forth for the cocktail party round.

Then there are those fiendish flat dinner parties, when the candles burn down and the ill-assorted guests, a farmer, a male model and a stockbroker, are forced to make stilted conversation until a revolting dinner that wouldn't disgrace the Borgias is served up three hours late.

But there are good moments: setting off for the fray in a shared taxi, which smells like a summer garden from everyone's scent, or those manic sessions at two o'clock in the morning when you all come back a bit tight from different outings and shriek about your experiences, until the old boot in the flat below starts tapping on the ceiling.

And it's somewhere to live even if the rent is high and the landlady's a nosy old bag, and you can always find a new flat or new flat-mates. For the Guardswomen of Chelsea have one aim in life, they're looking for a husband as hard as the landlady is looking for the rent.

FIANÇAYS: TROUSSEAU'S CONFESSIONS

"*Orange blossom is quite the Fox's brush of Female life.*"

SURTEES

The Fiançay can be forgiven for being a little smug. From the age of four she's been worrying about whether she's going to get married or not; now the Beechers Brook of her life has been cleared. The temptation, however, is very strong to kick her in the teeth as she sits about holding her hands in such a position that everyone notices the sapphire set in two diamonds flashing on her finger, beginning every sentence 'Gideon says', and lecturing her unmarried friends on the inefficiency of their sex lives.

"Daddy says I must be vacant to get engaged."

Her smugness will be short-lived, she will be far too busy in the weeks before the wedding making lists, writing thank you letters, being photographed for the *Tatler* with a soppy expression on her face, dragooning bridesmaids into frightful dresses and coping with their tantrums afterwards, coping with her father's tantrums because none of the younger generation are answering invitations, and worrying that senile Uncle Willy will expose himself at the reception.

She will also be looking drawn from pre-wedding crash diets, practising wedding night shrieks and praying that Gideon will believe that story about her losing her virginity on the tennis court.

It's to be a quiet wedding with eight hundred guests, three bus-loads of tenants, and 'Sheep may Safely Graze' at the entrance of the bride.

NEWLY WEDS

"YOUNG WIFE: *I've been trying to figure out where my husband spends his evenings. Last night I came home early, and there he was.*" JACK HULBERT

Newly weds are pretty smug when not collapsing from exhaustion. Supposed to look dewy but usually have bits of sleep rather than stars in their eyes. Spend their lunch hours shopping and struggling home with bulging carrier bags, which usually collapse just as they're getting out of the tube.

"We've only been married four weeks two days and five minutes," they say with a coy giggle. "We still celebrate our weekiversaries."

Up until now people have referred to them as Honor and Norm; now they'll be called the Longbottoms, or the Cheviots, like a range of mountains.

WIVES

Wilt! Thou hast this woman for thy wedded wife.

When a man asks if he can bring his wife, you can be sure she's a beauty or a battleaxe, he's either proud of her or too scared to leave her behind.

Super Woman is perfection as a wife, her house is always spotless, her husband's shirts laundered at home, "because the laundry do them so badly". Although she does a full-time job, she is able to give intimate little dinners for her husband's business clients once or twice a week, type out his reports, watch his calorie intake, rev up in gold lamé every night in bed, yet be up to cook his breakfast, and hand him his briefcase and umbrella as he sets out for work. All her girl friends detest her.

"My husband only has eyes for me," she says smugly. Eyes maybe; presumably the sensible fellow keeps his member for someone else.

Super Woman is always flirting with her husband in front of other people. It looks bad: as Oscar Wilde says, rather like washing one's clean linen in public.

UNHAPPY WIVES

"*The best part of married life is the fights. The rest is merely so-so*" THORNTON WILDER

Unhappy wives have dreadful clothes. What with school fees and Norman's philandering, they can't afford to buy any new ones.

"She's let herself go dreadfully," say her friends, then add mystifyingly, "What she really ought to do is really let herself go, and find a lover."

"*I'm letting myself go—goodbye!*"

The marriage is now in injury time, each party in its separate hell; the only sexual kick the couple get is out of rowing with each other. They always talk about having "stuck together because of the children", as though the little blighters have been using glue and sellotape on them.

FIRST WIVES

People tell me snakes are not dangerous to handle, and that they are not slimy but cool and dry, but my flesh still creeps when I see them. It's as impossible to expect a second wife to like a first wife, as it is a wife to like a mistress. The latter will always be a threat, albeit an imaginary one, to the former. And yet curiosity draws them together. Women who love the same man have a kind of bitter Freemasonry.

When first wives meet up with their first husbands they annoy the second wife by indulging in an orgy of name-swapping about people they knew in the old days.

One first wife, when she sends her children to stay with the second wife, includes a list of their clothing to be ticked off like a school list when they come home.

Other than praising her children, the quickest way to endear oneself to a woman is to say diabolical things about her husband's first wife.

STEPMOTHERS

An archetypal bitch, the most unpleasant character in literature, who visits all the imagined sins of the first wife on any of the first wife's children. Can often be seen at cocktail parties grumbling: "Of course, Gideon refuses to see any of her faults, but what can you expect with a mother like that."

Stepmothers alas are here to stay, because even though the concept of the large family is declining, it flourishes in other directions: "Well, Gideon's got three fiends from a previous marriage," you'll hear a wife saying. "And I've got three angels from when I was living with Alaster, and Gideon and I've got two between us, so there's quite a crowd at weekends."

Someone should write a saga of the seventies called the 39 steps.

Third wives usually get on very well with first wives.

Fourth wives usually get on very well with second wives.

PREGNANT WOMEN

The pregnant woman is supposed to have a glow about her and to have never looked better. A fantasy built up by women's magazines. In fact she's a write-off from the sex appeal point of view after the fourth month, a sort of neuter, who wears her dresses eighteen inches higher at the front than the back—dresses she expects to wear afterwards as "little tops", whereas in fact they are more like the Big Top, or a marquee that could house the whole neighbourhood.

Pregnant women sit with their legs apart and have swollen ankles, which is probably what is meant by pregnant paws. Most of them are in love with their gynaecologist, and spend their time feeling their babies kicking like full-backs.

Plain women like being pregnant because suddenly they become 'interesting' and men, terrified they're going to explode, treat them like Dresden. Many women seem to believe there is some merit in suffering, and disapprove of any pain-killing methods. One woman I know insisted the midwife left the door open so her husband could hear her screams and know what she was going through.

If a woman gets pregnant immediately after she's had a baby, everyone clicks their tongues and blames the husband for being a dirty beast who couldn't leave her alone.

Sexual Norm's wife Honor is in a complete muddle; her friends come forward with an avalanche of advice on looking after the baby, all conflicting. The battle rages between the bottle boilers and the non-boilers, disposable nappies, Harrington towels, the Nappy Service and kidney-shaped safety-pins. Everyone gives her wildly differing lists on what she'll need. Sexual Norm thinks a Layette is a very small Nymphomaniac.

Honor tries to read baby books, but the page always falls open at vomiting or green motions. Sexual Norm enjoys the section on the Husband's Reactions: "It says I'm going to feel very left out," he reads happily. "And be grumpy towards you and spend more evenings with men friends and flirting with other women."

"Three safety pins, a marble and about 50p in loose change, and you said he wasn't eating."

LOVELY YOUNG MOTHERS

Milton, thou should be sterilising at this hour.

Young mothers have sick on their shoulders, go round with bags of equipment like plumbers, sigh continually, have very long ears from listening out for crying, and look as though they haven't slept for weeks, which is true. They spend their time pinching their babies to see if they're awake, and crying into the washing machine. They sterilise everything and would sterilise their husbands if they could.

Most women fancy the concept of themselves as lovely young mothers. As a girl friend of mine once said: "There was I with Tarquin and Crispin on my knee, hoping she'd say what a lovely picture the three of us made—and she didn't."

UNMARRIED MOTHERS

"*You don't think Jennifer'll do anything foolish?*"
"*Oh she's always doing foolish things.*"

Supposed to be the heroine of our time. She is now called a one-parent family. People say quite untruthfully that there is no stigma attached to being an unmarried mother. Actually she can't win. If she goes out to work people accuse her of depriving her child of its only source of affection, if she stays at home she's accused of living off the state, and the social security ladies come nosy-parkering round looking for thick woollen socks and Y-fronts on the clothes line.

It is only easy to be an unmarried mother if you can afford a nanny and a lover.

Unmarried mothers, according to their mothers, always get pregnant the *first* time they sleep with a man. They have a bitter look like women prisoners, live in hostels, and are understandably hostile. Married women sometimes employ them as nannies, automatically assuming they'll be wildly grateful, then start worrying that the unmarried mother will favour her own child rather than the employer's children.

BARREN LADIES

Women who can't have children worry continually that their in-laws and parents will develop complexes about being a grandchildless couple. They are also terrified of getting a dog in case people assume it is a child substitute.

Trying to have babies is a most dismal process. Most infertile women have worn a furrow down Harley Street, picketing gynaecologists, having five D and Cs, four salpingograms, and 500 cwt of ironmongery inside them. There is also the tedious business of taking one's temperature every day, and then having to pounce on each other when it goes up, which is always the morning you're late for work, or suffering from debilitating hangovers, or simply not fancying each other. Then a fortnight later, getting wildly excited because the curse is half an hour late, then feeling like committing suicide when it finally arrives.

If you ask a woman at a party if she's got any children she either says No—and there'll be a long embarrassed pause before she adds: "But I've got lots of godchildren, and I adore my five little nieces." Or she'll say no, then add hastily, "But we've only been married eighteen months."

If you can't produce children, people automatically assume you're undersexed. Society on the whole is quite sympathetic, but on the other hand rigidly disapproves of couples who can have children, but choose not to. Everyone will chunter disapprovingly about "selfishness" every time they eat out in a restaurant, buy a picture, or take another holiday abroad.

Super Woman is always giving herself heirs.

MISTRESSES—THE OTHER WOMAN

SHE: *Are you sure your wife won't mind about us?*
HE: *You'd better be careful, she's already killed five ladies and one platinum blonde.* EXECUTIVE SUITE

At one time kept in back streets, now flaunted in posh restaurants, mistresses have smooth marbly limbs, fur counterpanes and mirrors on the ceiling.

"George, are you coming or going?"

They also carry chisels and hammers to prise their lover loose from his wife.

Mistresses always say they're having an affair with a married man not a husband, and then add: "His wife's frightfully unattractive, a bit 'com' too; he's done so well since he married her, but she hasn't 'grown' with him."

The Kept Woman is usually the well kept woman, frightened of growing old and losing her figure. She complains: "I've given him the bust years of my life."

Her life consists of lunches, a few stolen hours after work, everything quick, nervy and watch-checking. She seldom gets her lover to stay over. Come midnight, he's out of her flat like a shot. He's probably frightened of seeing himself first thing in the morning in that overhead mirror.

Mistresses are always free at Christmas and Easter and are at a loose end at weekends, but, alas, loose is the last thing they get the opportunity to be.

One couple I know decided to be civilised and

asked the husband's mistress to a cocktail party they were giving. The mistress, who was tall, slender and beautiful in a deathshead way, chose the middle of the party to make her entrance. Approaching the wife, who was small and terrier-like, she bent down to proffer her cheek saying:

"Darling, how lovely."

A second later she leapt back, hand to a bleeding cheek, crying: "You bitch, you bit me."

GAY DIVORCÉES

"No desire to get married—it would take an awful lot of butter to get me into the frying pan again." GYPSY ROSE LEE.

You're only middle-aged once.

Gay divorcées wear big hats, gold pants, dark glasses and diamonds big as glacier mints. They have cleavages like the Grand Canyon, roulette chips rattling round at the bottom of their bags, and have never done it in the back of anything except a Rolls Royce.

They're just the sort of women to get schoolboys through A level Sex, and about whom Oscar Wilde said: "She has at least a dozen pasts and they all fit."

Gay divorcées never have to buy their own scent, and have voluptuous figures upholstered in black net—sort of mattresses en titre.

BEAUTIFUL DESERTED WOMEN

Born in Hazlemere
Schooled at Cheltenham
Courted in Kensington
Married in Chelsea
Bliss in Fulham
Parted in Tears
Divorced in Putney

Putney is teeming with beautiful deserted women rattling round in seven-bedroom houses, with two or three children. They have a forlorn air about them like a glove hanging on a hawthorn tree—no good without a partner. Most of them are impossibly overworked, going out to a job every day, coping single-handed with all the bills and mortgages, bringing up the children, and having to stay home from work jeopardising their jobs if one of the children is sick.

Their friends say tactless things like: "Henry's getting a bit spoilt, he needs a man about the house."

Meanwhile Henry's father takes him out at weekends, and returns him loaded with presents, nevertheless claiming he can't afford 50p. a week more alimony.

Other friends say Poor Honor's going through a very bad Patch, as though she were having trouble with a naughty mongrel.

It is very difficult these days for deserted women to get married again unless they break up a marriage. Unattached men in their thirties—apparently emasculated by the demands of Women's Lib and the emancipation of women generally—either seek the company of dollybirds who look up to them, or go queer out of spite.

As a modern novel said recently, "We've lost more men to homosexuality than we ever did in two world wars."

"I've been deserted."

The beautiful deserted woman is usually asked to dinner parties to make up the numbers with a queer or someone's husband down from the north. When men take her out they assume she must be screaming for it, as she's been used to regular sex. It is almost impossible for her to refuse to sleep with men—she's not given a second virginity to save for her second marriage, and if she says no, men go storming off into the night in a huff.

MAIDEN AUNT, MAIDEN ENGLAND

"*On the occasions when Aunt is calling to Aunt like mastadons bellowing across primeval swamps and Uncle James' letter about Cousin Basil's peculiar behaviour is being shot*

round the family circle—(Please read this carefully and pass on to Jane)—the family have a tendency to ignore me."
P. G. WODEHOUSE

Aunts are the salt of the earth; they're close enough for you to tell them things that would shock or hurt your parents. When you're about sixteen they ask you to call them by their Christian names. Awful women ask their friends' children to call them Auntie.

At weddings older aunts wear pull-on felts and wedding-cake crumbs on their moustaches and charge round spraying incesticide on any relations who get the least bit familiar.

BACHELOR GIRLS

"A woman with fair opportunities and without a positive hump may marry whom she likes." THACKERAY

People always assume that bachelors are single by choice and spinsters because nobody asked them. It never enters their heads that poor bachelors might have worn the knees of their trousers out proposing to girls who rejected them or that a girl might deliberately stay unmarried because she didn't want to spend the rest of her life filling a man's stomach with food and washing his dirty shirts.

Invariably bachelor girls are referred to by their families as Poor Norma or Poor Honor, and one can understand why they go home so seldom, when their parents' eyes are so full of questions they daren't ask.

If a girl gets married too young, everyone assumes she's pregnant, or the marriage will break up in a few weeks, or she's such a rabbit she can't wait until she's older for regular sex. Between twenty and twenty-six is quite acceptable for a girl to be still single; after that parents get a bit shelf-conscious, and start saying defensively: "Jennifer hasn't got time to think of marriage, she's got this very important job at the Ministry—absolutely J.B.'s right-hand man."

In a few years' time they will be hinting that J.B.'s relationship with their daughter isn't quite so platonic.

"I know if J.B. weren't quite so devoted to his children he and Jennifer . . ."

Then J.B. leaves his wife and elopes with a guardsman, which blows that one sky high.

An awareness of their parents' desire to get them married and the sight of all their girl friends with husbands and children often panics single women in their late 20s or early 30s into disastrous marriages. This is a vital time not to lose one's cool. It seems unfair, though, that so many women get divorced and remarried a number of times; and some of us don't get a chance at all.

When women get married over thirty they seldom wear white—it somehow doesn't seem fitting to flaunt one's lack of experience.

MOTHER-IN-LAW

"*Behind every successful man, there's an astonished mother-in-law.*" RICHARD NIXON

Princess Anne's got married, so they've got to make do with you.

The great mistake with a future mother-in-law is to assume she must be lovely to have produced anyone as lovely as 'him'. You roll up starry-eyed to meet her, forgetting that for her you're just the end of a string of girl friends, and she doesn't like your pedal pushers and sequinned shirt worn to impress his teenage sister, and your hips (because he likes you thin) aren't childbearing enough.

'She'll be extravagant," she's probably thinking. "Will she cook and mend and watch his weight, will she be the sort who rushes back to work the moment she has a baby?"

One of the troubles after marriage is that mothers-in-law only meet daughters-in-law when one of them is absolutely dead with exhaustion. When the mother-in-law comes to stay, the daughter-in-law sweats her guts out bulling up the house, trying to prove to her mother-in-law that she's keeping her son in the style to which he's accustomed. Then the mother-in-law arrives two hours early to find the house in chaos, the joint not in the oven and the children in their pyjamas.

Equally, when one goes to stay with one's mother-in-law she's absolutely knackered cleaning out spare bedrooms and cooking for five days ahead.

"I've run out of animals," said my mother-in-law despairingly, wondering what on earth to feed my husband's sister and her family on after they'd been staying a week.

Don't be misled by the fact your husband bitches about his family. That's his privilege, and he won't be amused if you do the same yourself.

Learn to play bridge, said one woman's magazine, the hardest rind conceals the sweetest fruit.

THE CHANGE OF LIFE

They're changing lives at Buckingham Palace.

Men are always supposed to be the nicer sex, because they get on so much better together than women do, but I think it's a miracle any women are on speaking terms at all, as fifty per cent of the time one of them will be suffering from pre-menstrual tension.

As my housekeeper says, God was in a cranky mood when he made women, what with the curse, childbirth pains, post-natal gloom, pre-menstrual tension, all sorts of gynaecological capers, and finally the change of life as a last act, and not all that well written at that.

How old is she? people ask. About thirty-seven, comes the answer, and everyone nods knowingly, and mutters, The Change.

Must be hell, all those hot flushes like geysers in New Zealand, drenched sheets and going red as a radish. It's not much compensation either, the way women's magazines are always rabbiting on about not having to take the pill any more, and the joys of mature sex, and the quiet serenity of the older woman.

The mother's change of life often coincides with her daughter's adolescence, but the daughter invariably gets blamed for being difficult.

Women going through the change of life often pretend their daughters are older than they are so people will gasp, and say: "You couldn't possibly have a daughter that age. I thought you were sisters."

OLD LADIES

Old ladies live with other older ladies whom they bully shamelessly, not because they need a companion but a sparring partner.

Rich old ladies drench themselves in lavender water, and at Christmas their relations subject them to arselick and old lace in the hope of inheriting some cash.

Poverty-stricken old ladies have a frightful time, sitting with only one bar of the fire on, and buying dog scraps from the butcher for a dog they don't possess. They do have some compensations, they can travel free on buses, and if they live alone in Camden Town they are entitled to a free budgerigar.

The real poverty in fact is in ourselves. For not looking after them better.

WORKING WIVES

Usually filled to the brim with resentment, encouraged by their mothers, who keep saying "You must

"Dog's got in again, Mum."

get so tired darling, and why doesn't Norm ask for a rise?"

If a man leaves his wife and goes off with another woman and his wife is not working, society blames her for becoming a cabbage and getting bogged down with domesticity; If she is working they blame her for neglecting her husband and not providing him with hot dinners.

Ladies and Sport

CRICKETERS

Women cricketers have divided skirts, long white socks, heaving aertex bosoms, broken fingernails, and spend their time emitting raucous cries of: "Well stopped, Daphne."

"*Wide? What d'you* mean *wide?*"

All have names like Whoopsy Daisy and drive sports cars. They are a disgrace. A friend of mine once described Tampax as a long stop between two short legs.

"Straighten those arms and let's get our tummy off the floor, shall we?"

KEEP FIT LADIES

Have black semicircles underneath the armpits of their blue denim shirts and don't get enough sex at home. Oh fit white lady who nobody loves.

LADY ATHLETES

Are pumped full of drugs and have strong sinewy legs. If you produce a dildo or a vibrator, they will attempt to run relay races with it.

HORSEY GIRLS—WHEN LOVELY WOMAN STOOPS TO FILLY

Go to any stables or horse show and you will find a Humbert Humbert's paradise: hordes of nubile girls wearing boots, expressions of innate superiority, and staggeringly tight breeches, their mousy hair rippling down their backs. Slightly bolshy, they would rather muck out than muck in. Most of them are in love with Graham Fletcher, and less snooty than they look. They never talk about anything but horses and take Equi-Librium to stop themselves getting over-excited.

"Well, I think it should be called the chest stroke, Charlene."

SWIMMERS

All called Little Nan Ray, they have oiled muscular shoulders, no busts, one-piece bathing dresses, run to fat and are touched up by disgusting old coaches in white flannels with watches round their necks. They also have bloodshot eyes, separated eyelashes, smell of chlorine and blow their noses in the water with their hands. When it comes to marriage they have no difficulty in taking the plunge.

RUGGER WIVES

Deserve a chapter in Foxe's *Book of Martyrs*. If they're not washing rugger shirts and having their best suitcases stolen to accommodate revolting towels and rugger boots, they're freezing on the touchline crying Come on Company, their faces turning purple and red like a mandrill's bottom. Alternatively, they can spend all afternoon chopping lettuce, and scraping paste made from prawns and other fish on sliced bread and marge, and bitching about the other wives who haven't turned up to spread.

Later they're expected to make a warm half of beer last all evening—even if you wash shorts, you're not allowed to drink them. Rugger wives more than anybody have mastered the art of sweating out a drink.

They don't have sex on Friday night, because their husband is keeping his eye, if nothing else, in, or on Saturday because he'll be too drunk.

Much of her time will be spent answering team secretaries (when her husband is two-timing his own team by playing for some other team with a ludicrous name like The Wasps), and saying most unconvincingly that her husband's been away on business all week, and won't be back from the trip until after kick-off on Saturday.

Newly weds usually come every week to Rugger matches during the first year, and say Gideon's wonderful, he never puts it in crooked. After that they turn up less and less frequently.

Super Woman always breezes in with two featherlight sponges filled with butter icing and asks if she can have the tin back. Everything would be very different if all rugger players looked like David Duckham.

The Arts

"Haven't you got any jeans, dear?"

LADY MUSICIANS

L'Après midi d'un phoney

There are no women of genius, they are all men. A statement borne out by Virginia Woolf's description of Dame Ethel Smyth rehearsing in "A short skirt, a workmanlike jersey, a battered felt hat, a flat chest, a drip on the end of her nose, and a powerful baritone voice, echoing through Portland Place."

Lady instrumentalists ride the cello sidesaddle, toss their heads a lot, and are inclined to be scruffy. Opera singers run to fat, and embarrass their children by singing Wagner in what they imagine to be sotto voce on station platforms. The only compensation is you can never hear the words.

ACTRESSES

Worry continually about bad breath, spend their

time resting and can never be rung up before lunch-time. They seldom have parts of either kind; "there is no work about", and most actors are queer.

LADY NOVELISTS

Good listeners because they're always on the look-out for copy. They justify their nosiness by saying it was Proust's curiosity that made him a great writer.

Lady novelists usually wear too much face powder so it clogs in the cleft of their noses, lipstick on their collars, and biro marks on their pillows and dresses. They are no good at sustaining relationships with men, but this is all to the good because every ghastly let-down is the silver lining of being able to write about it afterwards.

"Before the Police arrive I think you ought to tell me *all about it."*

Mixing often with queers, they are sustained by syrup of fags. They have large bottoms from sitting down so much, untidy houses, and seldom use a hair-brush or have varicose veins.

They are often found in bookshops surreptitiously moving their own books up to the top of the pile. They keep going to the loo at parties not because of weak bladders but merely to feed their nosy parking metres, and write down the latest witticism on the back of their cheque books.

When they tell you who they are, you've never heard of them. They pretend to have been very unhappy at school.

ARTISTS

Lady painters are mostly members of the behind the door school. Should stick to painting their faces.

ARTISTES

Sing 'Pale Hands I Loved' at geriatric concerts.

STUDENTS

Crinkly hair, college scarves, hunched shoulders, with so many chips on you get splinters if you pounce on them. Tend to fall in love with one-sonnet-a-year poets, who they fiercely defend as geniuses, wash their hair once a month, and have cats with hysterical names out of the classics, and posters on their walls of two hands coming out of the lavatory. Later they become Graduates and wonder if it was all worth it.

GRADUATES

Never capture the first fine careless rapture when they were the toast of L.M.H. Particularly in Oxford and Cambridge where the men outnumber the girls, they get an inflated idea of their own sex appeal and often marry very attractive men out of their own sexual hierarchy. Marriages which break up later.

Having graduated they find to their horror that they have been prepared to do precisely nothing, and after taking a typing course which is far more of a headache to them than a school leaver of sixteen, they get a job in publishing at a thousand pounds a year.

They have a permanent air of not being wanted, which is true. The only thing for them to do is to take other degrees, grumble and despise other women who aren't graduates. In their houses are rush mattings, and copies of the *T.L.S.* and the *Listener* unread.

Sometimes they resort to gardening and cooking, which is as far as their creativity will stretch.

Kinsey quotes that between fifty and eighty per cent of academic women never achieve sexual satisfaction, so they're a bit cross about that too.

Female Types

"*Mr. Foster, I* never *cross my bridges until they eventuate.*"

DUMB BLONDES

"*How do you manage to do so many silly things in one day?*"
"*I get up early.*"

Like sex symbols, dumb blondes are out of fashion today. In the old days they had huge busts, and said things like: "Oh look, that seagull's just excruciated on the deck."

Now most of them are brunettes who have lost all their exuberance, keep their cool, never utter, and get a reputation for being mysterious, which men erroneously believe will lead to frenzied fanatical bedroom payoffs.

JEWISH MOTHERS

Beyond reproach, since they've given the world so many marvellous people. Tend to be a bit overpossessive. A Jewish girl friend of mine told me she and her husband had made love on the bathroom floor the other night. "How romantic," I said, "after you've been married ten years." "We can't screw in the bed," she said. "Daniel sleeps with us."

Daniel is five.

LANDLADIES

Premises. Premises.

TORY LADIES

Wear petalled hats in summer and pull-on felts in winter; have ringing voices, grey short perms, open pores, closed minds, refer to the lower classes as 'them', but consider themselves very democratic because "I get on awfully well with my Mrs G." Their Mrs Gs refer to them behind their backs as "bossy boots". They're always talking about "approaching the mayor or the local tradesmen", as though they're going to sidle up and tweak them on the nose.

Much of their time is spent waving tins at street corners and giving long sentences. They have flat bottoms from sitting on so many committees, and flat feet, for trampling on people. (They wouldn't want anyone to escape under the arches.) When they go shopping they pull baskets on wheels with copies of the *Daily Telegraph* inside.

TRENDY LEFTIES: NON-U-TOPIA

Radical chicks. Always getting up petitions, and

organising community centres with their own theatre workshops. In spite of being very rich, they insist on sending their children to state schools, but buy large houses in areas where the state schools will be most populated with middle-class children anyway. Trendy lefties drive round in foreign cars, have colour television and bang on about the evils of consumerism. Conscious of the world population problem, they are thrown into a complete panic if they get pregnant with a third child, and contemplate having an abortion or going to the country to have it, in case other trendy lefties find out.

When you visit them they say: "The kids will be down in a minute," as though a herd of goats is about to come stampeding down the stairs. Their children are bright, but have the most frightful accents, which they pretend not to mind about. They have playrooms rather than nurseries.

They dislike animals but keep neurotic dogs, because they've read somewhere it's good for children to be brought up with animals. They speak with accents, but occasionally forget and when angry or frightened can talk with quite posh voices.

COUNTY LADIES

Summer County, Some are County, some are not.

Upper-class ladies always wear their hair off their foreheads, and their skirts on the knee at exactly the right height to be goosed by large gundogs. Whereupon they say: "He can smell my dog on me."

Upper-class ladies have clean eyes, country-life

faces, wear dung-coloured clothes, and can be heard from three acres away. Much of their lives is spent beating bracken, walking hound puppies and displaying large tweed bottoms in the herbacious border. They have houses in Scotland, shotgun honeymoons rather than weddings and all know each other.

Conversation is limited to Dutch elm disease, lake draining, wildlife parks, and the servants who are never in the right house at the right time.

They are not snobbish and the most damning thing they would say about another woman is she's the "Sort of gel who wears shocking pink in the country."

They don't get much sex from their husbands. There is a story about an ancient peer who woke up for the first time in years with an erection.

"Shall we inform her ladyship?" said the butler impassively.

"No, no, Treadwell," said the Earl. "Let's smuggle it down the back stairs and take it up to London."

ZOO-MANIACS: THANK HEAVEN FOR LITTLE GULLS

Earth-box mothers, who fill their houses with animals, tend to be indifferent to men. They prefer the uncritical adulation of an animal who will never answer back and will adore them whether their hips spread or red veins proliferate on their cheeks.

They usually have houses that smell like the zoo, not a hare out of place, and furniture upholstered in ginger fur. They never wash up, cats' little tongues being far more abrasive than any pan-scourer.

Their motto is love me, love my dugs.

SLUTS

Sluts wash their hair once a month, have goaty armpits, gorgonzola feet, nails filled with eyeshadow, and laundry baskets pulsating like compost heaps.

One slut I knew never washed her pants, only ironed them. You can imagine the steam that rose off that.

When men help them on with their coats they always put their arms down the lining and can't get their coats on.

Herrick as well as hustling virgins has a lot to answer for on the slut front too.

"A sweet disorder in the dress kindles a kind of wantonness," is the slut's motto, and a marvellous excuse for uncombed hair, laddered stockings and dresses welded together with safety pins.

Sluts are always panic-stricken when they lose their bags, not because there's any money in them, but because someone might discover the mass of bus tickets, hair, clogged make-up and 55 mascara brushes inside.

Twice recently where women's magazines have asked if they could photograph the contents of my bag, I've had to go out and buy a new one, and fill it with completely new things. On the most recent occasion I only just stopped my husband filling it with dog biscuits and strange auto-erotic devices.

"I regret having to inform you, Miss Gordon, but we have incinerated your underclothing."

Sluts wear their hair over one eye because they're too lazy to pluck both eyebrows, have very weak arms which makes them deficient in elbow grease, and wash up with fingers and cold water or their husband's flannel.

When they get married, and sluts always do because they're quite capable of cleaning themselves up during their courting days, they have houses decorated by runny-nosed brats and unemptied chamber pots.

DOILY BIRDS

Prissy prissy maiden.

Very refined, they come wrapped in cellophane complete with their own pedestal. They always sit in cars like stuck pigs until the driver runs all the way round and lets them out, can't be sworn in front of, and screw their faces into 'neat gin' expressions when people tell filthy jokes.

When asked what they'd like to drink they say just a sweet sherry, and when asked if they'd like another one they put their hands over the glass.

When doily birds go to the loo, they rustle paper all the time, lining the seat so that no-one can hear anything. They keep their Tampax in blue plastic holders. They tend to wear Laura Ashley dresses, ribbons in the hair, Peter Pan collars and six pairs of knickers, and talk about fourheads. Their children wear frilly knickers over their plastic pants, and ruched bikini tops at the age of four.

"So important to be feminine," says the doily bird, throwing herself on to her husband's knee, and talking in baby talk.

She also says 'Cos' and 'Comfy' all the time, has a voice like Katie in the Oxo ads, wears colourless nail varnish, and lays a doily under her husband before he gets into bed. She and her husband often call each other Mummy and Daddy.

At mealtimes she serves up aeroplane food, which looks better than it tastes. Everything in the fridge is in plastic containers.

"Foiled again," says the paté dispiritedly to the cheese.

My brother and his wife once had a doily bird to lunch and gave her a mixed grill including a kidney. Too refined to say she didn't like offal, she slipped the kidney into her hand and held it there through the rest of lunch. Finally after lunch they went into the drawing room, and my brother maliciously enjoyed watching her edge towards the fire and when she thought no one was looking flick the kidney into it, whereupon it let off the most terrible hiss.

WOMEN'S LIB LADIES

A Ms is as good as a Male.

One of the most heinous crimes of the twentieth century is to say all Women's Lib Ladies are ugly and Lesbian and only Libbers because they've been hurt and can't get it together with a man. Certainly looking at those brawling aggressive Coven-fresh harpies who attend Women's Lib meetings or represent the movement on television, one would be forgiven for thinking so. While one sympathises with many of their aims, one can only deplore the stridency and violence and whining with which they try to enforce them.

"I tell you Women's Lib needs all the support it can get."

Although they are always agitating for equal pay, they get very uptight if men don't get up when they come into the room or expect them to pay for drinks. They are always complaining about women being exploited as sex objects, but we never hear the sex objects themselves complain.

At parties Sexual Norm, who is suffering from Suffragette Lag, is often asked how he stands on Women's Lib. To which he replies: "I'd like to jump up and down on them."

Men who support Women's Lib actively are always extremely wet.

COSMO GIRLS

The complete antithesis of Women's Lib Ladies. All sex objects, they have bouncing curvy figures, rub baby oil into their bottoms every night, and exercise their vaginal muscles in the bus queue. They are all gourmet cooks, size ten, and produce the same candlelit recipe every month. They read the newspapers every day and are terribly understanding about impotence or premature ejaculation. Most of them are having far too exciting a time in their jobs and being Olympic level in bed, to settle down until they're at least forty. With so many Cosmo girls floating around it's surprising the rest of us ever get a man at all.

SMALL WOMEN

Have a tendency to tweeness, and say "I'm only a

little 'un" and make a hell of a row so they don't get lost at parties.

Apart from making one feel like a carthorse by comparison, I've always detested small women since a boy friend, after staring at me for about half an hour, said: "Gosh, you'd be heartbreaking if you were tiny."

"I said, Miss Marriott, there isn't a tall tree that can't be climbed."

TALL GIRLS

Stand about at parties looking gentle and apologetic like Great Danes. Women's magazines are always exhorting them to play up their height with high heels, so they bang their heads on the ceiling, and to wear bold dramatic prints so they can hook bold dramatic princes.

GROUPIES: PHALLUS IN WONDERLAND

A teenage friend tells me that "promiscuous" is a word that doesn't exist any more, because everyone is. Groupies are girls that specialise in sleeping with pop singers, which can't be much fun. They are inhabited rather than inhibited, wear non-stick frying pants and have eyes that don't drop quickly enough but knickers that do.

In America really classy groupies decorate their walls with plaster casts made of their own private parts and the members of famous pop stars they have slept with. Flying Fucks rather than ducks, I suppose.

COUNTRY GIRLS

Have pink cheeks, flat shoes, clean underwear, and an innocent but healthy attitude towards sex, having seen so many animals copulate and give birth. When they visit London they're easy to pick out because they're so much more done up than anyone else.

TOMBOYS

Tomboys have ruffable hair, freckled faces, scarred knees from climbing trees, big nipples, small breasts, and often go as men to fancy dress parties.

"I was a terrible tomboy at school," is the cue for long boring reminiscences about how naughty they were. They refer to their boy friends as "my chap" or "my bloke", and like being spanked for sexual kicks because it recreates the stormy relationship they had with Miss Pickersgill at school.

THE BRICK

A brick is the sort of girl you fall back on rather than forward onto. She's the good sport who doesn't mind being blown to bits in cars, or freezing on the touch-line, and is happy to go dutch and drink half pints. She reads the sports pages, and does the *Telegraph* crossword in half an hour, inking out the clues as she goes. The Brick drives her own car, which she lends to men to take out prettier girls, and is always left to do all the cooking when she goes sailing. Men treat her very badly. They often mean it literally when they say in the pub: "I dropped a frightful brick last night."

"I say—steady on old girl."

STEADIES

Girls who are going steady walk round with their arms round their boy friends as though they were running in a three-legged race but had forgotten to tie their inside legs together. They spend a lot of time gazing at each other in doorways, and will say, "We go out on Tuesday, Thursday and the week-end." They eat very slowly when they go out, because as they're holding hands they have to cut up their meat with their fork. They are inclined to produce creased photographs of the beloved, and say: "It's a terribly bad one of him."

WOMEN'S WOMEN

"Gosh, there's this marvellous girl at nursery school, Alexander's madly in love with her," raves Honor to Sexual Norm. "She's got a super figure."

Women regard super figures as being thin; and sex appeal as having a pink and white complexion, regular features, a glint-free eye, and being generally wholesome, rather like girls that introduce children's television programmes.

MEN'S WOMEN

Who ever loved that hated not at first sight.

The ideal sex partner gives promise of a good tussle. The more animosity she harbours the better. She is the opulent tigress, the bitch goddess with a 38 bust, a very narrow back and endless legs, the man-hater who is bashed into fawning submission by the hero in the last chapter. Helen of Troy—the most beautiful woman who ever lived—was very fond of wrestling.

BEAUTIES

"May she be granted beauty and yet not,
Beauty to make a stranger's eye distraught,
Or hers before a looking glass . . ." W. B. YEATS

The beauty has a design-centre sticker on her bottom, and sends men's hands fluttering like butterflies to straighten their ties or smooth their hair whenever she enters a room.

One automatically thinks of Lady Diana Cooper or Polly in *The Pursuit of Love*, the sort of woman one can't stop gazing at in the pathetic hope she might have gone off in the last few seconds.

Most of the beautiful women I know are, most unfairly, extremely intelligent, but somehow they seem to spend so much time primping, looking at themselves in the mirror, going on diets and having stormy affaires that they never seem to do much with their lives. Like Ming vases, they are beautiful but empty. As a result they have frightful hang-ups about being just a pretty face, and the quickest way to get them into bed is to tell them you admire them for their minds.

Most women admire beautiful women and get a certain kudos having them as friends. Women often indulge in pointless conversation about whether people are pretty, sexy, beautiful or attractive, fishing like mad for the other person to say: "Of course you're all four."

MODELS

Models have difficult pregnancies, high tight self-assured bottoms, and moustaches drawn on them in the tube. They are often filmed drifting through the buttercups in a nightie or performing fellatio on a bar of chocolate. They retire at twenty. Most of them have their teeth fixed, so they're capped women rather than kept women, and manage to smile dazzlingly and keep their eyes wide open at the same time. In bed they are like skeletons.

Whenever a man takes a model out he always describes her as a top, never a bottom model. They do not have brains and say y'know, funtastic.

NURSES

Monstering Angels

Nurses are very smug because all their patients think they're absolutely wonderful. They have a profound contempt for anyone outside the medical profession. They always know too much.

Quite unshockable, they prefer men horizontal to vertical. Night nurses are at home all day, and therefore a good bet for married men.

NANNIES

Have a terrible life, living in other people's houses as part of the family, yet not part of it. Every time they try to discipline the children the mother drifts in and messes everything up. Parents assume that Nannies get so frightened of getting fond of the children that they must move on every few months. Actually, they get sick to the teeth of the parents.

We've been through every kind of Nanny: the sexy towel-slipping variety, one who ate cheese all day and used to bath in the dark, another who set fire to the drawing-room twice and turned the dog into an alcoholic, another who had black men in all night, another who wanted to be a nun and kept discussing her heavy periods with my unfortunate husband. Another looked like a ferret, and my husband used to make ferret faces behind her back to make me laugh; another ran up fifty pounds of grocery bills on my account.

When I interview them now, after telling them about the colour television in their rooms and the run of the telephone and my husband, I add: "I'd like you to stay at least a week."

CONTINENTAL GIRLS

When I was a gel, foreign girls used to be considered the only people who knew anything about sex, but today English girls have easily outstripped them.

As one Spanish au pair girl said: "When they came to my country I thought, Oh well, they're on holiday letting themselves go a bit. Now I'm in England I see they're like this all the time."

Swedes are supposed to be all sex maniacs, to bath in Badedas and to be Bad for Dad. French girls have an innate sense of superiority: they're like Old Etonians—not necessarily superior, they just think they are. Spaniards have very hairy legs, and however much they shave, bristles stick through their stockings like Mrs Tiggy Winkle.

"On Sunday efeninks eet is elk yoursel'."

Sexual Norm has a German au pair, and keeps them in stitches in the local saying: "The trouble with my house is that it's over krauted."

AMERICAN GIRLS

Hygienic with the light brown hair.

All cheese dipsomaniacs. If you go to drinks with one you'll be prevailed upon to plunge bits of raw carrot and cauliflower into disgusting goo, and given such strong martinis, you'll feel too sick to have any dinner.

Americans are useful at parties because they always say Parm Me when they're introduced to anyone, so you catch the names the second time round.

They regard Europe as dreadfully dirty. "The English have more wax in their ears than they have on their tables," said one American.

Most of them are going to analysts, have plastic private parts to withstand a deluge of vaginal deodorants, and go in for Caesarian births:

"To keep your toobes honeymoon fresh."

Older American women—the Blue Rinse Brigade—charge round Europe wearing plaid and plastic concertina headscarfs to keep off the rain, and give cries of anguish at everything old.

A member of the Blue Rinse Brigade and her husband visited an English peeress recently. The husband, who was called Elmer, sat in bootfaced silence during the whole visit, but as they were leaving the wife said "So nice socialising with you, Lady X. I have nev-urr seen El-murr so animated."

Afterwards Lady X went back into the drawing room and found a vast box of chocolates lying on the sofa, as big as the sofa. On top was a card printed with the words:

"To the loveliest lady we know."

American intellectuals differ from English intellectuals, in that as well as being clever, they are often beautiful and extremely good at cooking and running a house. They use so many long words, it is difficult to understand them. They call their bags 'pocket books'.

LESBIANS

Very fashionable at the moment. As a reaction against the coolness and narcissism of the young men today, girls are dressing up in men's suits, cutting their hair short and wearing trilbies like Lulu.

The world is supposed to be teeming with unrecognised Lesbians who look like everyone else. Men are rather keen on the idea, and have fantasies about watching two Lesbians in bed together, but they visualise two lovely young things with trembling golden buttocks, rather than two hoary old frumps with monocles and Eton crops thrashing around like dinosaurs.

Women are often described as Practising Lesbians as though they spent seven hours a day at it, like musicians.

NYMPHOMANIACS

Chaps with Everything—Here comes old Knickerless Nickleby.

Supposed to be Lesbian or frigid, might be very tired and want to lie down all the time, or be doing market research into mattresses.

Nymphomaniacs have for hire signs on their foreheads, mad eyes that look as though they've been swimming under water too long, sandpaper vaginas, and the acceleration of an Aston Martin towards anything in trousers. Their approach is to sidle up and say: "I've got a bottle of whiskey at home."

I used to know a nymphomaniac called the Garrison Bicycle because everyone rode her. She was supposed to be impossible to satisfy and men went off gland in hand into the sunrise.

My husband has always wanted to meet a nymphomaniac; he says the ultimate rejection would be to be turned down by one.

WHORES

All hands to the Pimp—my orifice is my fortune.

Tarts have hearts and parts of gold.

Respectable women kid themselves that prostitutes are all old bags (or American old pocket books) or Lesbians who hate every moment of it. But some of the ones I've met have been ravishingly pretty and were having a high old time.

One man I knew went to bed with a tart in Hamburg and was charged the equivalent of £190. He paid by American Express.

A friend who had a wooden leg was driving down Park Lane before the days of the Wolfenden Report, when an enormous negress put her head through the window and said: "Want to come home with me?"

To which he replied: "What, all the way to bloody Africa?"

TEASERS

Chaste are the ears
Although the eyes are rogues. LA FONTAINE

Teasers grin but don't bear it, they want to attract men and bask in their admiration, but not reap the consequences. They will not sin for their supper.

Prickteasers flirt and tease, chatter and giggle, produce a force-ten gale fluttering their false eyelashes, and are always brushing imaginary crumbs off men's trousers, knowing they have already thrown the keys to their chastity belt in the river.

Prickteasers say "Oh go on," and don't mean it.

"Your oats were in the porridge, Hamish."

SCOTSMEN (see Tory Ladies)

They wear pleated skirts on the knee and their bushes outside. Their wives are full of beans and bairns.

INDIAN LADIES

You undress them by unbandaging them; often they unravel themselves and take nude photographs in instant machines on railway stations. They make disgusting carrot pudding, and always take everything you say seriously.

FRIGID WOMEN

She'll be coming round the mountain when she comes—singing Ay Yay Yippy.

With all the books on female sexuality pouring off the presses, I would have thought it was virtually impossible for a woman to be frigid these days. More controversy rages over the location of the female orgasm than ever did over the source of the Nile. Whether you're in the clitoris or the vagina camp, if you don't achieve multiple orgasm every time, you feel one of the flops of the decade.

Like the pathetic letter in *Forum* recently:

"I've never had the smidgeon of an orgasm and sherry doesn't help."

A famous beauty who's kept more lovers happy than I've had hot dinners told me she's always been frigid:

"I just wriggle about and pretend."

People are always saying about frigid women:

"She's got two children, she must have done it twice, ha ha ha ha."

Frigid women who have saved it for marriage are determined not to spend it all at once. They dawdle over their baths, and are horrified when they read in sex books that lots of men are still leading vigorous lives in their eighties.

It seems a pity, if you don't like sex, that you can't hire someone to sleep with your husband. After all you employ a Nanny to look after your children, which is one of the traditional wifely functions.

NEUROTICS

Valium is the better part of discretion.

PIN-UP GIRLS

"*You must not forget the suspenders, best beloved.*" KIPLING

Gatefold nudes have staples through their stomachs, are the colour of Red Indians, have double-barrelled names like Mary Blanche-Maison, live in Sussex and read Greek at Oxford.

Pin-ups are usually photographed in high heels, stockings and suspender belts, jewelry, big hats and newly set hair, as though they were arriving at a smart society wedding, but had forgotten to put on their dresses. Although they often appear to be lying down, they are in fact photographed against a wall so their breasts don't go fe-lop. If they are photographed with pubic hair it's known in the trade as beaver; if they have their legs apart it's called split beaver, which upsets both Mary Whitehouse and the R.S.P.C.A.

OLDER WOMEN

"*No spring nor summer beauty has such grace*
As I have seen in one autumnal face." DONNE

When I was a teenager I thought middle age started at thirty, but as I get older it starts later and later, as the end of one's shadow gets further and further away as nightfall approaches. Ever since my thirty-first birthday I've got out of bed every morning, peered at my naked body in the mirror and said, not bad for nearly forty.

Older women spend too much time looking for liver spots on their hands, and crêpe on their thighs, and wondering whether they ought to cut their hair short, buy an all-in-one foundation garment, start making love in the dark, and turning off lights and sitting with their backs to the window.

They also try very hard to be gooder and have a better sense of humour because it's supposed to show in one's face after forty.

What is the older woman's role in life? Does one give up sex altogether, or will one's future be initiating shy schoolboys and boy scouts into the mysteries of mature love? They're so precocious these days, they're all having each other at twelve anyway.

The most important thing is not to be a nuisance. Ageing women who throw themselves at men imagining they're still young and beautiful are like my dog after he's swum in the muddy river or rolled in manure, who then bounds up expecting everyone to pet and adore him just the same.

It seems sad that society disapproves so strongly of women having affairs with younger men. I suppose it all stems from the ability to produce children. After forty a woman is not likely to provide her young lover with lusty sons, whereas the older man is perfectly capable of giving a lovely young thing a baby up to the age of eighty.

Women and their Pastimes

HOUSEWORK

The call of the running tidier.
The glory that is elbow grease.

Few tasks are more like the tortures of Sissy-fuss than housework, the clean being made dirty, the dirty clean. Houseproud ladies spend their lives ferreting out fluff from under beds, sponging fingerprints off their husbands, and moving ashtrays half a degree nor-nor-west. They also have Jay cloths permanently at the ready. All they think about in the Spring is cleaning, and when you hear them having intense discussions about fast coloureds and delicate whites they're talking about their washing machines not about sex.

Nowhere does Parkinson's Law operate so efficiently as in the house: mechanical gadgets don't cut down the time spent, they just mean you wash sweaters after you've worn them once instead of scraping the food blob off with your fingernail, and that you feel honour bound to make mayonnaise in the mixer rather than getting it out of a bottle.

Most housewives, Women's Lib tell us, work an eighty-hour week, and therefore get slightly irritated when people say:

"What do you do?"

"I'm a housewife."

"What do you *do* with yourself all day?"

Or when their husbands say smugly "Oh my wife doesn't work."

Their status is consequently sustained by a spotless kitchen and by raising housework to an art form.

"Get off Roger—the sheets were changed this morning."

The whole scene is fraught with problems. On the one hand you read magazine articles warning you that the battle against decay is a denial of life, and that marriages break up because wives are always flapping dusters. Or that children's lives are very short, and how glad you'll be you let the washing-up pile up that Wednesday and spent all day making doll's clothes.

On the other hand you have vague worries, as you trip over a child's bicycle in the hall or look at your toy and nappy strewn kitchen, about the Greek love of order and beauty, and how men loathe muddle, and that behind every really successful man is a clockwork wife.

I think women do all that sighing and ferocious tidying and banging about of pans at weekends to show their husbands how hard they work and because they're panic-stricken that the place won't be tidy enough when the char turns up on Monday morning.

GOSSIPING

Here comes lovely Mrs Cooper—the soul of indiscretion.

Women seem to find it necessary to spend half the day on the telephone talking at 10,000 words a minute to their friends. Men get furious when their wives gossip on the telephone: "You get so silly," complains my husband.

He also gets wildly irritated when I closet myself with female relations on family weekends and indulge in the usual indignation meetings:

"High time that dog went to prep school . . . and what about Uncle Tom's Cabin boy . . . so selfish of Alison to have only one, large families bring each other up." (Like cannibals, I suppose.)

TONGUE CLICKING

Another favourite hobby is clicking the tongue, pursing lips and poking one's nose into other people's business. Old crones in fawn herring-bone coats do it individually, shivering the net curtains every time you go out without a bra or talk to anyone who isn't your husband; or throwing up windows and complaining every time you give noisy parties.

Angry Mothers, a collective body much publicised by the newspapers, are always working up states of fury and clicking their tongues over the school lavatories: "These toilets are disgusting . . . definitely."

"George, but how do you know *the fridge light goes off when the door shuts?"*

WORRYING

Women are not happy unless they've got something to worry about, usually the size of their bust, or losing their looks. If more than one woman are gathered together with rapt expressions on their faces and slightly watering mouths, they're talking about:

SLIMMING

"There will be too much of me in the coming by and by."
W. S. GILBERT

'Flu and falling in love are the only ways to lose weight, both a bit of a nuisance if you've got a husband and children.

"I eat sensibly," says Super Woman, "I watch my figure."

Honor eats insensibly. Two drinks and she doesn't care any more: "Must have something to blot up the alcohol," she says, diving for the canapés.

Next morning the Woman's Page will be advocating post-holiday slimming diets because they've got nothing else to write about. And Honor will be aware of her trouser zips plummeting and seams splitting. She will vow not to buy any more cheap clothes, and wonder if her trousers could possibly have shrunk at the cleaners. She then leans backwards and forwards on the scales to make them weigh lighter, does her trousers up with a safety pin which gives more leeway than a hook and eye, and wishes nostalgically she'd lived in Edwardian days when our great grandfathers drooled over fleshy ladies.

One of the difficulties of going on a diet is the revolting things you have to eat—grapefruit without

"*Well the lettuce may be* out *of the garden but it's* by *every cat in Barnes.*"

sugar, vegetables without butter, and undressed lettuce. It's no wonder you feel very bad-tempered and think about food the whole time.

Anyway fatness per se isn't unattractive, it's just the voluminous black sweaters, and tunic tops, and heavily made-up face to detract from the blocky figure, that is.

As soon as Honor loses weight she starts wearing all the clothes she looked too fat in before she lost weight, and so looks exactly the same.

THIN WOMEN

I eat like a horse.

Nothing is more irritating than thin women who are always going on diets.

"Can't get into any of my clothes," they say, ribs pushing through their unisex blouses. "I just cut out potatoes if I gain a few pounds."

The Cosmopolitan Doctor, who can't enter into any correspondence, says latent homosexuals go for very thin girls like Twiggy, and men who are looking for their mothers go for fat girls. So take your pick.

SHOPPING

Nothing brings out the gladiatorial spirit more in women. They make out ludicrous shopping lists: 3 spanish navels, 2 Comforts, 1 large Pal, 2 small Chum, one Tom pureé, then disappear into vast chain-stores and ferociously crash their steel trolleys against one another.

God knows why they're called supermarkets, as there's nothing super about them. One spends far more than one intends to and by the time some pink-overalled crone has finished jabbing away at an adding machine one discovers one hasn't enough money for everything.

When middle-aged ladies come to London, they

head straight for Marshalls, and have lunch with their daughters, who work as "sekketries". Believing their daughters never eat properly in London, they force on them a vast meal of a glass of sherry, tomato soup, plaice fried in breadcrumbs, fruit salad and white coffee.

Afterwards, the glass of sherry having gone to their heads, the mothers buy several good wool or 'semi-evening' dresses, come home absolutely exhausted with too many carrier bags and say they could never live in London. They then hide the carrier bags, and bring out one new dress a week to show their husbands, lying about the price.

CLOTHES

Men never quite understand why clothes are so important to women. "What does it matter what you wear?" says my husband, after at least six dresses have been tried on. "No one's going to look at you anyway."

"That's what I'm afraid of," I mutter.

Women buy most of what shows off the best part of their anatomy. Women with good legs spend a fortune on shoes, those with good busts spend fortunes on sweaters. Before I married I used to buy a new dress every week; it was considered death to romance to be seen in the same thing twice.

Jackie Onassis used to spend £16,000 a week on her clothes. Onassis was absolutely delighted when with superhuman effort she cut down to £8000 a week.

HATS

Women put on special faces when they try on hats, pursing up their mouths and opening their eyes very wide.

When I was seventeen I remember changing in the school train to meet a boy friend to go to *South Pacific*. I wore a pair of grey suede shoes, a bright emerald-green coat, and a black straw hat with a veil and a red rose on the front like a miner's lamp.

We had lunch in a Chinese restaurant, and I had great difficulty eating through the veil—bits of Chop Suey kept getting stuck.

Everyone stared at me, I remember, and I assumed it was because I looked smashing, but it must have been because I looked such a fright. As is the case with most hats, you get stared at rather than fancied.

In Yorkshire there's a saying 'Red hat, no knickers,' which always cheers one up when one sees a bossy Tory lady in a red pull-on felt. Poke bonnets are worn by girls who want to get poked.

SEAMSTRESSES

Women spend a lot of time and *angst* dressmaking. I used to come home and find pieces of stuff all over the floor, and my mother with her mouth full of pins talking exactly like John Wayne. Quite often she would cut out two left fronts. By the time she had finished the garment, she was usually so bored, and my father was so bombed with: "It does look all right, doesn't it darling?" that neither of them could ever look at it again.

"If it was all right for me, it's all right for you, Griselda—anyway the forties are back in fashion."

Occasionally she would make clothes for me which caused frightful arguments as she would never make things tight enough in case my bottom or bust stuck out too much.

DROPPERS IN

Women have numerous ways of amusing themselves. One is dropping in—rolling up at nine o'clock in the morning with the baby and the dog and the carrycot for a gossip, then standing round watching you do housework, so you have to wash the glasses in separate water and can't taste the cooking too much, or blow your nose on a drying-up cloth.

Others turn up with a bag of maggoty windfalls, say how's the babe and try and rope you in for what my son calls 'jungle sales'. These women are usually

"It may be a fine time to drop in, Mummy, but actually I've dropped out."

described as saints, which means they have big feet, and never wear make-up or bitch about people. Saints tend to have large families of sons who hug them in the kitchen and say: "You're the only woman in my life, Mum."

They go to early service on Sunday then ring you at 8.30 when you're in the middle of making love, saying: "Sorry to bother you so early, but I knew you'd be up, having children."

COFFEE MORNINGS

Women also feel it is important to get on with each other during the day, so they give coffee mornings, which are sheer purgatory—cocktail parties without sex or drink. After coffee and gâteaux you discuss a book you've all read, recommend time-saving products to one another, discuss baby's difficult bottom and play word games.

One woman was asked to think up the name of a

part of the body named after an animal. The answer was actually Hare, but she was thrown out for writing down Pussy.

HOLIDAYS

When women go on holiday, even for a day trip to Boulogne, they spend three weeks packing and buying up the entire local chemist because they don't trust any of those foreign medicines. Rows occur at sporadic intervals, after Honor's ruptured the bathroom scale with her excess baggage, or, if they're travelling by car, because Sexual Norm refuses to stop on the endless autoroutes for anything but petrol.

When they finally reach their destination, Honor is irritated that all her crease-free dresses have creased, and her Carmen rollers and her travelling iron won't fit into any of the sockets.

That night Honor goes out in her holiday uniform of a sleeveless dress and a white cardigan and expresses horror at all those little children drinking wine. Next morning she spends even longer getting ready for the beach than she would for a ball. By evening she has had too much sun, and all she wants to do after two bottles of wine at dinner is to go to bed at 10.30. This happens most nights of the holiday but she still grumbles because Norm, irritated by not getting enough sex, hot foots off to the casino every evening and blues all their savings buying whiskey at 100 francs a tot for some French tart.

As the holiday goes on, Honor looks permanently

as though she's just come out from under the dryer, and she has to wear looser and looser flowered orlon tops to conceal her spreading hips. She and Norman have also met up with an English couple and both couples feel honour bound to retire to bed for three hours every afternoon in case the other couple should think them undersexed.

Honor lies on the beach and wishes she could have a slim brown figure like those French girls reading *Elle*. She wishes she hadn't had three croissants for breakfast, and vows to skip lunch. Then she sees all those slim brown girls tucking into great loaves of bread and salad niçoise and decides to have some too.

"Just think! In 24 hours it's home and half a grapefruit a day only, for the next three months."

The way to *Elle* is paved with good intentions.

Before they go home Honor and Norm have a row because Honor wants to spend the rest of their money buying presents for the children, her daily woman and her mother, and Norm wants to spend it on the tart at the casino.

SKIING

Occasionally women go skiing, come back glowing with health and clean up at winter cocktail parties, because everyone else is the colour of bacon fat. As soon as the men get them home and rip off their clothes, they discover these girls are also the colour of bacon fat except for their faces, and lose interest. To try and win them back, the girls give revolting Glühwein parties, show slides, and try to re-create the atmosphere of the châlet.

OLD GIRLS

People who go back to old girls' reunions were usually in the hockey eleven or prefects for whom the world never recovered its magic after they left school. Everyone is very hectic, they all blow in and out, and rock the room with gales of laughter and reminisce about jokes in the dorm and the crush everyone had on Miss Pickersgill.

Honor, who was not a success at school, looks at all her contemporaries and secretly hopes she doesn't look as old as that. They are all doing the same to her.

She finds herself talking just as obsequiously to the muscle-bound frump who was captain of hockey, as she ever did when she was at school.

Looking around at the eager unpainted faces, the whispy hair, the baggy skirts, she's amazed so many of them have married. The uniform seems to be lots of cardigans, fur-lined boots, an inch of petticoat showing beneath the skirt, and a large beret of neutral-coloured felt pulled down to one side.

GREAT GIRL FRIENDS

Women spend hours talking to their friends on the telephone saying How's so and so, he's fine, and how's so and so, and she's fine, and how's etc. etc. She's a *great* girl friend of mine, they say, so you imagine some huge amazon walking through the door. Women like women for different reasons than men do: they can get very attached to humorous boots, girls at work, girls next door with whom they can discuss nappies and the price of fish, none of whom are likely to appeal to their husbands.

Honor finds she has to smuggle in the friends Norman doesn't like. "Marion might just possibly pop over after lunch on Sunday," means she's actually invited Marion to dinner.

When pretty friends come to stay, Norm is very accommodating, and only too happy to fix their bedroom light after everyone else has gone to bed, take them early morning tea, and drive them to the airport.

Intense loyalty to one's girl friends is an excellent let-out when you don't fancy the husband:

"Oh I couldn't possibly do it to Honor," cries Honor's best friend.

Norman, who has fantasies about three in a bed and both of them doing it to Honor, is very disappointed.

When women want to escape from each other at parties or in the street they say: "We must have lunch sometime."

"No, I bloody well won't point the car in the direction of the map!"

WOMEN IN CARS

Young girls generally kick their shoes off when they drive cars, say 'sugar' when they grind the gears, and tend to go forward in a succession of jerks. If they go to a party in their car and meet an attractive man, they pretend they've come in a taxi on the chance of getting a lift home. A pounce is worth a parking ticket.

They regard cars rather like washing machines, and deliberately refuse to take any interest in what goes on underneath the bonnet.

Men fancy girls in sports cars, but dislike being driven by them except when it means missing valuable drinking time.

How often at a party you see a woman sourly sipping tomato juice and the husband happily swilling whiskey "because Jennifer's driving".

HOSTESSES

Let us now prise out famous men.

As opposed to great girl friends, hostesses are always

described as "little". They have at home cards printed with their names on so they can just add the date, write down what they gave people last time, and invite names to meet names, who never ask them back.

Once upon a time before the advent of Robert Carrier and Elizabeth David, one could go out to dinner and not die of indigestion and hangover the next day. Now it's all gourmet cooking, cheese before fruit, three different kinds of wine and wafer-thin mints.

Norm thinks it's called Cor-may cooking, because he always says, "Cor, may I have some more." He describes Honor as a Cordon Bleu cook, which is a euphemism for any old tat served up with so much cream and wine and garlic in everything you wake up burping at three o'clock in the morning.

Super Woman takes half an hour to give a dinner party. The silver and the plates are all clean anyway and she has only to whisk five courses out of the deep freeze, or whip up a quick suprême de leftovers.

Honor takes two days, most of which are spent racking her brains over the placement, which she used to think was some kind of liver. Can you have two queers sitting next to each other, and does a mistress take precedence over a catamite?

She is so anxious not to have a last-minute panic that she cooks everything hours ahead. Norm is sulking because he can't have a bath, the bath being full of ice cubes. Honor changes into her hostess gown, the sleeves of which trail in the gravy.

The guests arrive. She has left at least three-quarters of an hour for drinking before dinner, and only a quarter of an hour has gone and Norman's boss's wife, who doesn't drink, is already looking bored. Norm's friend One Night Stan has arrived drunk and is already telling dirty stories.

"Ronald, don't mention the béarnaise again—there will be savoury scrambled eggs for pudding!"

After two gins and tons, in spite of cooking ahead, Honor is desperately trying to uncurdle a last-minute sauce, keep the toast, now the consistency of flannel, hot, light the candles, and remember to put out the butter and open bottles. Norman having read somewhere that either the host or hostess should stay with the guests, is sticking resolutely to the drawing room.

Honor, who knows a gracious hostess makes a relaxed party, is trying to prise a jammed crust out of the toaster. A smell of burning fills the house.

Now they sit down to dinner, everyone sticking elbows into the next-door neighbour's eyes whenever they help themselves. Norm's boss is getting very excited over One Night Stan's wife, but no one is talking to Norman's boss's wife, who is looking bootfaced. Honor jerks her head to the right, hoping everyone will turn and talk to the guest on their right, but no one does, so she does it again and again, and succeeds in cricking her neck.

The beef, which has been cooking in Châteauneuf du Pape for 12 hours, is completely tasteless. Guests push it to the side of their plates saying 'That grapefruit really filled me up.' Later they fall upon the cheese.

Norman, having cracked his head on the low-slung Christopher Wray lamp last time he got to his feet, is refusing to fill up anyone's glass.

Everyone suddenly jumps out of their skin, at the pneumatic drill shriek of the coffee grinder.

Honor gets graciously to her feet.

"Shall we go upstairs?" she says to the ladies.

"Yes please," says One Night Stan leaping to his feet and following her.

SEX

"*To make love without feeling a particle is sad work and sad and serious did I find it.*"

"*Everything's getting on top of me these days except Henry.*"

Hot on the trail of gourmet cooking comes gourmet sex. Today people start getting hang-ups if they don't have sex beautifully served up three times a day with a piece of parsley on top.

Honor wakes up on Sunday and wearily ticks off all the things that have to be done:

(1) Norman
(2) The children's breakfast
(3) The ironing
(4) The dog's breakfast
(5) Sunday lunch
(6) Norman

It amazes me how couples with young children ever make love at all. Thank God for *Catweazle* or *Doctor Who*, which at least gives you a clear childfree half hour. It should be re-christened family screwing time.

Honor, worried about hers and Norm's sex life and making heroic attempts to improve it, has been reading a book called *How to Improve your Man in Bed*, which tells her she must practise removing Norman's clothes "without clumsiness or hold-ups and preferably with one hand". But who does she practise on?

She is also told to acquire some sexy underclothes. She buys a garter suspender belt which slides down over her bottom the moment she puts it on and makes her new black stockings wrinkle. Another suggestion is to treat Norm to a strip show. She removes her bra as they're going to bed, and waves it round like a football rattle. Norm asks her if she's been at the gin.

Norm is even more worried when Honor, again acting on the advice of *How to Improve your Man in Bed*, moves in the builders to knock down the bedroom wall so they can have a bathroom adjacent to the bedroom, and "not lose any sexual heat running down long cold passages". The builders are shortly followed by the painters to re-decorate the bedroom in more intimate sexy colours. The bill is staggering,

"Right—Catweazle, Treasure Island, Dr Who and then Golden Shot and not a sound for the next two hours."

and there are more bills for Honor's school-girl outfit from Daniel Neals, a new double bed, and a huge looking-glass for the ceiling. Norm always believes if you take care of the penis, the pounds will take care of themselves.

Other hints on lovemaking include:

"Tying each other up." (Norman feels Honor bound and then goes off to the pub.) "Throw his pyjamas in the dustbin." Norm is livid, his pyjamas were new, black with red piping, and what's he going to walk round in now when his mother-in-law comes to stay?

"Never tell him Jim was better. Get all dolled up for an evening and tell him you've forgotten your pants." (Norm is horrified and tells Honor to go upstairs and put them on again.)

"Offer to fellate him at odd moments of the day." (She'll get a clip over the ear if it's during "Match of the Day".)

"Make the most of morning erections, but eat apples first to sweeten the breath." (Poor Norman is woken from deep sleep by frenzied fiddling and scrunching, and grumbles he prefers his alarm clock.)

Honor gives up, throws *How to Improve Your Man in Bed* in the dustbin with one hand and goes back to the missionary position once a week.

In Victorian times, women were disapproved of if they enjoyed sex; today they feel guilty if they don't want it all the time. Sex is often the loveliest thing in the world, but people shouldn't feel guilty about having too much or too little. And feeling you ought is just as oppressive as feeling you oughtn't.

THE DATE

"Is it one of my well looking days, child? Am I in face?"
GOLDSMITH

At last One Night Stan rings. Sexual Norma, who has been biting her nails for weeks, drops her voice three octaves and says Hello. Stan asks her out, she says she might be able to squeeze him in, what about Monday, Tuesday, Wednesday, Thursday or Friday? After she puts the telephone back her voice reverts to normal and she shrieks: "He's rung, he's rung."

She then goes out and buys a completely new set of clothes, including a new pair of jeans and a bra to look as though she's not wearing a bra.

On the day of the date, she spends three hours at the hairdressers. When a mirror is held up so she can see the back of her head, she mutters gosh, yes, marvellous. When she gets home she brushes it all out.

She then spends another three hours getting ready,

rouging her navel, washing her ears and spraying scent onto her pulse spots, including the back of her knees.

The doorbell goes. She doesn't feel quite the million dollars she had hoped. A maddening piece of hair keeps sticking out at right angles, mascara has got into her eyes, her jeans, in spite of a 24 hour crash diet, are making her walk two inches off the ground, and even with layers and layers of Erace, a large spot on her nose is shining through like a lighthouse.

"Where shall we eat?" says One Night Stan when he arrives.

Sexual Norma can't think of anywhere except Claridges or Jo Lyons.

The next four hours are spent sipping cocktails, which go straight to Norma's head and other parts of her anatomy, dining by candlelight, dancing in a discothèque blacker than great Agrippa's inkwell, and groping in a taxi on the way back to Norma's flat.

Norma, who is feeling sick through too much drink, wonders if she asks Stan up whether she'll ever get rid of him.

"Would you like a nightcap?" she says timidly.

"Never wear them," says Stan, pushing his way resolutely into the flat.

They then express a mutual interest in gramophone records, and Norma plays a record which she likes because she knows it, but Stan doesn't like because he doesn't know it. One really shouldn't on the first date, says Norma to herself rushing into the bathroom, cleaning her teeth, drenching her bosom in 100 per cent proof, and putting an intellectual French novel by the bed instead of Barbara Carthorse.

Back in the drawing room, Stan puts his hand over Norma's, she puts her other hand over his, he puts his other hand over hers, Norma pulls out her bottom hand to put over his, and this goes on faster and faster until they are slapping each other's hands.

In the bedroom Stan starts to undress her, Norma complies—anything to get out of these crotch-murdering jeans.

Norma doesn't enjoy much of what follows; she tries to remember what *The Sensuous Woman* told her, but all she feels is her mother standing at the end of the bed waving an admonishing finger.

Afterwards she wonders how long she has to lie in simulated ecstasy before charging off to the loo.

When she returns One Night Stan is dressed and about to disappear into the night. For the first time that evening, Norma feels she'll mind very much if she doesn't see him again, and shouts after him, "You will ring me, won't you?"

Of course, he doesn't. Norma's flatmates sympathise with her, but in private they are delighted. They know men. It's all champagne and fairy tales until they've had their all, then you can't see them for dust.

LOVE

"*I said to Heart, 'how goes it?' Heart replied:*
'Right as a Ribstone Pippin!' But it lied." HILAIRE BELLOC

From smug middle age, it is very easy to be a little

patronising about the agonies of being in love. Often when waiting to hear whether something I've written is going to be accepted, I recapture all the ghastly twitchy uncertainty of a life ruled by the telephone. You know the sort of thing.

He said he'd ring in the morning and now it's five past one, perhaps he's cooling off. And three other men have rung and had their heads bitten off for not being him. And I've just had a cold bath in case I might not hear the telephone over the sound of the geyser. And just rung up the engineer for the third time to see if the telephone's working. Why the hell can't he telephone me so I can stop thinking about him?

Conversely, the moment you go off a man he's never off the bloody blower making a nuisance of himself.

Then there's the agonising rat race of getting men to marry you. As a girl friend of mine screamed at her boy friend the other day: "You haven't even given me a ring that I can give back to you." Or another girl I know who was walking her boy friend purposefully past a jeweller's window, when he paused suddenly and peered inside, his eyes lighting on a large and beautiful ring.

"I like that," he said gazing into her eyes. "Don't you, darling? Do you think we can afford it?"

"Oh, yes, darling," she said, trying to control her ecstasy.

He then went into the shop—and bought the ring for himself.

Then an affair breaks up, and one has to cope with one's friends in a state of uncontrollable misery.

"You'll get over it," you say feebly as though the sodden lump on the sofa was about to undertake the Olympic high jump.

One girl I remember going on and on all evening about how miserable she was, like a rat in a trap: "I love him," I heard her saying dramatically to my husband, "I love him per se."

"Who the hell's Percy," said my husband irritably, "I thought you were in love with someone called Paul."

PARTIES

We are three girls, we share a *flap*.

At girls' parties there are always too many men, at men's parties far too many women. "But you've invited ten extra girls," I wail to my husband.

"Doesn't matter," he says airily. "I can chat up at least five at once and so can Paul."

Girls in flats give parties either because they want to pay back all the men who've wined and dined them, or more usually because they want an excuse to invite a man they've always fancied but never got anywhere with. All the invitations go through the office franking machine, candles are rammed into bottles, and the sort of wine you wouldn't wash your car down with, is served.

If it's a cocktail party, all the men arrive first straight from work at 6.30, and you suddenly have 42 men and two girls. The girls who have gone home to change and tart up don't arrive until eight o'clock, by which time all the men have got bored and gone off with each other or to another party.

If you give an after-dinner party, all the women arrive about 9.30, so you have 42 women and two queers making overbright conversation, until the men arrive after the pubs are closed at 11 o'clock, often bringing girls with them. And finally your best friend goes off with the man who was the reason you gave the party.

ADULTERY

One crowded hour of glorious wife is worth an age without a name.

"For my part, when all's said and done I'd still rather be cuckolded than dead." VOLTAIRE

ALL WORK AND NO PLAY MAKES JACK ADULTEROUS.

I'd prefer not to know, says the reasonable husband. I'll kill you if you look at another man, says the chauvinist pig. The cuckolds in between—the majority—simply don't believe it.

Helen of Troy—a well known adulteress—allowed her husband Menelaus to wine and dine Paris for nine days. Under Menelaus' nose, Paris wrote "I love you" in wine on the table, seized Helen's cup and drank from the same part of it as she did, making sheep's eyes at her, and generally behaving in a very adolescent way. The moment Menelaus was out of the house, Helen pushed off with Paris, abandoning her nine-year-old daughter, who might have grown into competition later, but taking her baby son, several of the palace treasures, gold to the value of five talents and five of the serving maids. Last week, Honor's friend Diana went off with the dentist and the furniture. So times haven't changed.

Adulteresses of today always tell their husband they've been shopping in Knightsbridge, when he comes home in the evening and enquires why they weren't in when he rang.

"I tried on lots of things," they say airily, "but I couldn't find anything that fitted."

Adulteresses get home very late and flustered, and have to placate the au pair with bunches of flowers. Au pairs often have bedrooms like funeral parlours.

Adulteresses gaze at their lovers for hours in parked cars, find they can't book into hotels together unless they've got luggage, and out of opening hours spend a lot of time sitting in residence lounges drinking black coffee and saying No to trolleys of cakes. Even in Paris, hotels with three stars pretend to be puritanical to force the adulterer into booking a second room.

Honor is not very good at being unfaithful to Norm. One day she planned to leave the children with a friend, who suddenly found she couldn't take them. Honor then rang up her lover to cancel lunch and found he had booked a table in another name, and there were five Browns and four Smiths with booked tables.

When she arranges a home fixture, the window-cleaner keeps turning up and grinning at every window.

Women when they start an affair improve enormously in looks; their eyes shine, and their coat gleams as though they've just taken a course of Bob Martins.

"You should have seen her before I moved in," says the lover complacently.

Adultery has become very fashionable these days. It's now called extra-marital sex, and is regarded as a form of therapy: she'll perk up if she has a stint in another man's bed. Jealousy is very out of fashion, but there are an awful lot of bitten nails about.

WIFE SWAPPING

Everyone suddenly burst out swinging.

Wife swapping always seems to happen to other people. London says it all goes on in the country with reference to the hunting shires, the country says of course, it all happens in London; and both London and the country believe it all goes on in the suburbs with wall-to-wall housewives thrumming with lust.

Wife swapping seems so divorced from the caprices of genuine desire. Why should Norma be offered as a sacrificial lamb to another husband just because her husband fancies his wife?

There was a riveting piece in *Over 21* in which a married woman said: "Wife swapping is a sort of phase everyone goes through like pottery and golf. We're not bored with each other, just bored with the set-up. I think women who go round sleeping with other people's husbands in private are much worse."

"Well, it's been quite lovely meeting you Mr & Mrs Hartman but our baby-sitter gets quite upset if we're not back by ten."

In fact the wife swappers are just as prudish and rule-bound as everyone else. Norm for example can sleep with Gideon's wife, and Gideon can sleep with Honor when they're all together, but Norm isn't allowed to slope over to Gideon's wife in the afternoon for a quick bit on the side when the others aren't about.

Once you are a wife swapper, you are also supposed to keep quiet about it, and not tell any one in the outside world, as it will be bad for all the wife swappers' reputations. A sort of Honor among thieves, says Norm.

If there's a wife swapping session on a council estate or in a village, the wife always plays at home in case the children wake up.

How does the whole thing start?

According to *Over 21*:

"Usually people ring up and say come round for dinner—and you know what it means. Generally we start with drinks and a buffet supper" (everyone presumably starts buffeting into everyone else) and people disappear upstairs.

"Sometimes the host just says, well let's get on with it. But I do prefer something to eat and drink first. You can have four different men a night if you want to, but if you get sick of it, you just dress and chat, if you don't fancy anyone you needn't join it."

But imagine the Mammoth sulks if Honor refuses Gideon and five minutes later is found thrashing on a mattress with One Night Stan. And how awful if no-one wanted you. And what would one wear, instant tan all over I suppose, and something loose enough not to leave crease marks on your body when you stripped off. And would people start gossiping if you stayed with the same man all night?

Honor, ever loyal, tells the others:

"Norm's frightfully light on his elbows."

TROILISM

Tweedledum and Tweedledee agreed to have a battle-axe.